PHYSICIANS AND GLOBAL HEALTH

First published in Great Britain in 2018 by Little, Brown

Designed by Emil Dacanay and Sian Rance, D.R. ink

A CIP catalogue record for this book is available from the British Library.

ISBN 978-1-4087-0640-4

Printed in China

COVER: Halley research station, Antarctica (Richard Corbett)
PAGE 1: The medical facility at Camp Bastion (MOD/Crown copyright)
OPPOSITE: A British decompression chamber from the 1930s (Fox Photos/Stringer)

500
REFLECTIONS ON THE RCP 1518-2018

PHYSICIANS AND GLOBAL HEALTH

Krishna Chinthapalli

Royal College of Physicians

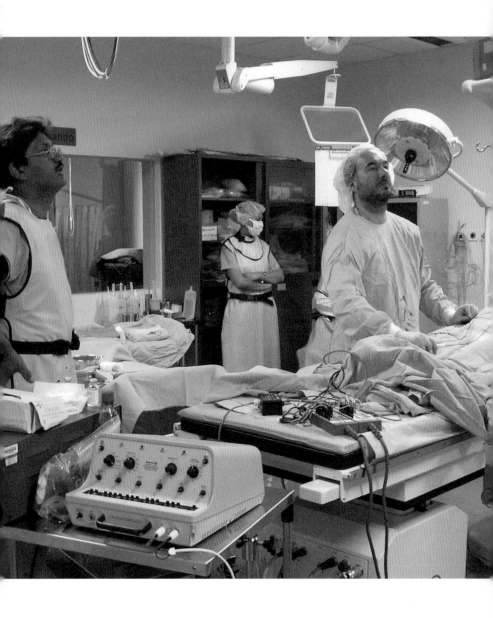

Prof David Martin and Dr Roy John perform radiofrequency catheter ablation procedure at Viedma Hospital catheter laboratory, Bolivia (©Project Pacer International)

FOREWORD

The Royal College of Physicians was founded, by Royal Charter, in 1518 by King Henry VIII. Few professional organisations have been in continuous existence for so long, and over its five-hundred-year history the College has been at the centre of many aspects of medical life. Its principal purpose is to promote the highest standards of medical practice in order to improve health and healthcare, and its varied work in the field is held in high regard.

As part of its quincentennial commemoration, a series of ten books has been commissioned. Each book features fifty reflections, thereby making a total of five hundred, intended to be a meditation on, and an exploration of, aspects of the College's work and its collections over its five-hundred-year history.

This, the last volume of the series, celebrates the international work of the College, and unlike its predecessors is focused mainly on contemporary activities. In recent years, with the globalisation of medicine and medical institutions, these activities have become an important part of the College's work. The MRCP examination is now conducted in 28 countries and 20 per cent of College members practise outside Britain. This book captures the range and excitement of the work of physicians in seven continents of the world. It has been expertly brought together by Dr Krishna Chinthapalli, who served as the NHS Medical Director's Clinical Fellow at the College and worked with his authors to provide this fascinating volume, and which serves as a tribute to all the physicians at the College.

I must also offer grateful thanks to all who helped in the production of this book, and especially to Maxwell Baker and Julie Beckwith in the Library and Museums section of the College, and also to Natalie Wilder and Professor Linda Luxon who have been intimately involved in the production of the series. As always too I offer grateful thanks to the freelance designer Sian Rance for her excellent work on all the books of the series.

Simon Shorvon -

Simon Shorvon, Harveian Librarian 2012–16, Royal College of Physicians
Series Editor

CONTENTS

ACKNOWLEDGEMENTS

Krishna Chinthapalli

I would like to thank Simon Shorvon for inviting me to write the final book of the series to celebrate the College's 500th anniversary. He fully supported this book on the global impact made by members and fellows of the RCP, past and present. I am very grateful to all of the contributors and their remarkable stories here.

In the College, many staff deserve thanks but I would like to mention three people especially. Julie Beckwith has been ever helpful and patient with my queries and Iain Fossey has given valuable suggestions and advice on current international activity. Max Baker has been instrumental in honing the design and content of the book.

Thanks to my wife, Moulika Atluri, for her support throughout. Finally, I would like to thank you, the reader, for your time and hope you find the book inspiring.

Nigel and Deborah Bax

Our first few visits to Iraq were supported by the International Medical Corps, a charitable organisation underwritten by the State Department in Washington. We are now supported by the British Council.

Most generously, the Ministry of Health in Iraq has given the University of Sheffield an office in Medical City in Baghdad. The Vice Chancellor of the University of Sheffield, Professor Sir Keith Burnett, and Ruth Arnold, the University's Head of Strategic Projects, have been most generous in their support of the work as has Sir Andrew Cash, Chief Executive of Sheffield Teaching Hospitals NHS Foundation Trust, and Dr Andrew Gibson, another College fellow, who is Deputy Medical Director in the Trust. Without their wisdom and help we would be nowhere.

David Martin

I would like to express deep gratitude for the support of Biotronik, Boston Scientific, GE Medical Systems, Hewlett Packard, Medtronic, St Jude Medical, as well as a number of New England hospitals. The provision of equipment, as well as the donation of a large volume of pacemakers and defibrillators has been in large part due to the sustained generosity of these industry partners.

OPPOSITE: A new ward at Yangon General Hospital, Myanmar (© Krishna Chinthapalli)

THE WORLD IN 1518
KRISHNA CHINTHAPALLI

Five centuries ago, the Royal College of Physicians (RCP) owed its very origin to the world outside England. As Henry VIII proclaimed in the RCP's founding charter, the King's personal physician, Thomas Linacre, had carried back the seeds of the idea from northern Italy. In turn, the College and its membership have been nurturing other medical institutions around the world, such as John Morgan's first medical school in the United States of America and the first medical school in Hong Kong.

Over the centuries, College physicians travelled around the world, including Hans Sloane's scientific expedition to Jamaica and Patrick Manson's customs medical officer post in China. If fellows of the RCP helped drive forward medical science, the fellows also held back social progress. Thomas Hodgkin (1798–1866), a Quaker, refused an invitation for fellowship of the RCP out of principle against its narrow-minded attitude to religious minorities. He also fought against the mistreatment of native people in Canada and of Jews in Morocco. For a century after Hodgkin, no woman was even allowed the chance to turn down fellowship. The first woman to join, Helen Mackay, had helped to reveal the cause of rickets and iron-deficiency anaemia from studying children in Austria in the 1920s. These physicians are featured as examples overleaf.

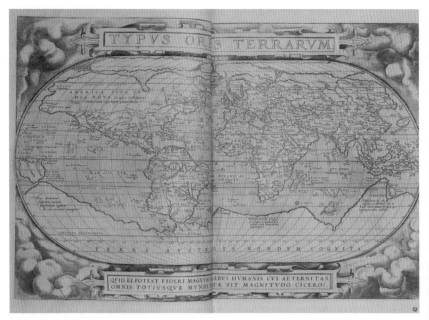

ABOVE: A map of the world from 1579 by Flemish cartographer Abraham Ortelius
OPPOSITE: The College's grant of arms by Christopher Barker, September 1546. (Both images © Royal College of Physicians)

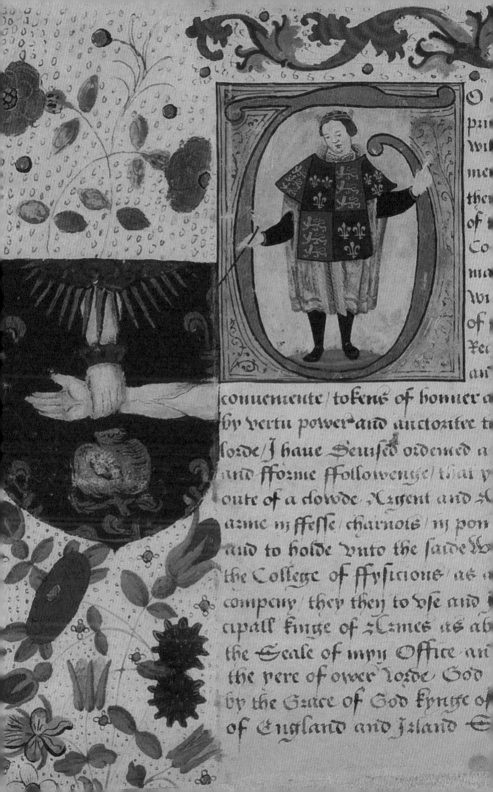

O
pri
wi
me
the
of
Co
ma
wi
of
te
an

conuenicute / tokens of honner a
by vertu power and auctoritee t
lorde / J haue Seuised ordened a
and fforme ffollowenge / that y
oute of a clowde Argent and A
arme in ffesse charnois / in pon
and to holde vnto the saide W
the College of ffysicions / as
company / they then to vse and
cipall kinge of Armes as ab
the Seale of my Office an
the yere of ower lorde God
by the Grace of God kynge of
of England and Island

OLD WORLD MAP

ITALY, IRELAND, JAMAICA, USA, CANADA, MOROCCO, CHINA, AUSTRIA

HUDSON BAY
1836 -1837

PHILADELPHIA
1735 -1789

KINGSTON
1687 -1689

The Second Borgian Map by Diego Ribe

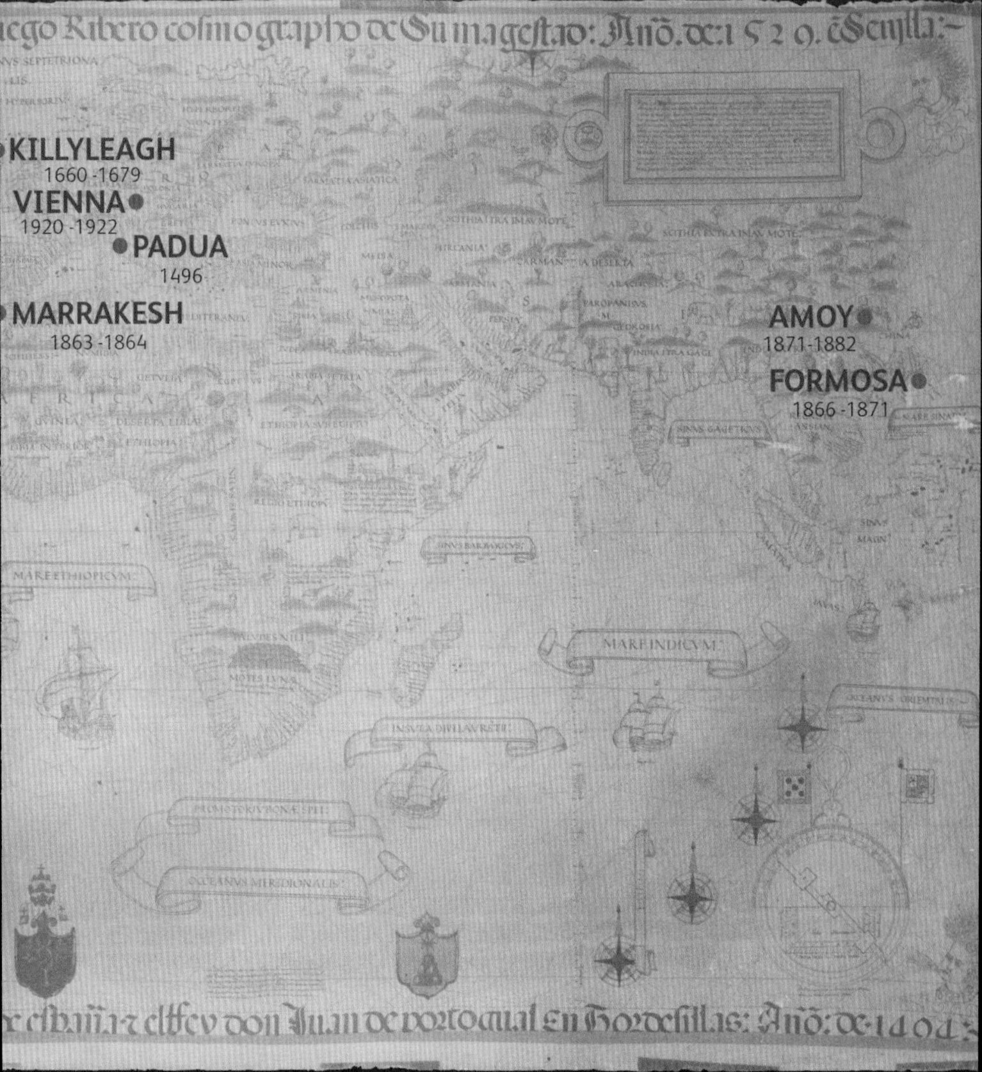

KILLYLEAGH
1660 -1679

VIENNA
1920 -1922

PADUA
1496

MARRAKESH
1863 -1864

AMOY
1871-1882

FORMOSA
1866 -1871

A 1529 map by Portuguese cartographer Diego Ribero (National Library of Australia/Wikimedia public domain)

PADUA, ITALY
KRISHNA CHINTHAPALLI

'Thomæ Lynacro clarissimo medico' ends the Latin inscription on Thomas Linacre's grave. *Medico* is the Italian word for doctor, and it is in Italy that the foundations of the Royal College of Physicians were built. Linacre, an Englishman, studied in Oxford and later travelled to Padua, which was described by those in Oxford as 'a most famous university for all humane studies'.

In Padua, the ancient university's standing was enhanced by the end of the 1400s thanks to generous donations from its Venetian rulers. A medical Renaissance began there with the translation of original works by the famous physicians of antiquity: Hippocrates, Galen and Ibn Sina (Avicenna). Linacre himself was the first Englishman to translate Greek medical works into Latin including Galen's '*On the use of the pulse*' – the very skill featured on the RCP coat of arms. Linacre graduated as a doctor of medicine in Padua and returned to practise in London, becoming the physician to Henry VIII in 1509.

Over the next decade, Linacre used his influence with the King and his Lord Chancellor, Cardinal Wolsey (to whom Linacre was also physician), to set up a society for medical practitioners. Linacre must have known of such an organisation of physicians, called a '*collegio*', existing in the Italian cities of Florence, Siena and Venice. He had realised that such a society would enhance the reputation of physicians, would distinguish them from the quacks and would allow physicians to meet and learn from each other. Indeed, the six physicians who petitioned the King would later meet in Linacre's own house on Knightrider Street near St Paul's Cathedral. He also expected that such a college could certify doctors. At the time, it was only bishops and other clergy who had the

ABOVE: Thomas Linacre, painted by William Miller in 1810 (© Royal College of Physicians)
TOP: Padua's anatomical theatre. (Kalibos/ Wikimedia public domain)
OPPOSITE: The RCP's charter, affixed with the seal of King Henry VIII (© Royal College of Physicians)

right to examine and license physicians in London and the provinces. That was to change in London 500 years ago.

In March 1518, three pages serving Henry died from fever. To escape their infection, the King fled to Richmond and then further away to an Oxfordshire village. New outbreaks of smallpox and plague were also spreading in London and Oxford. These epidemics concentrated the mind of Henry VIII and his courtiers. Thus, by September 1518, he granted a charter forming the RCP. His charter begins:

> *We have thought it to be chiefly and before all things necessary to withstand in good time the attempts of the wicked, and to curb the audacity of those wicked men who shall profess medicine more for the sake of their avarice than from the assurance of any good conscience, whereby very many inconveniences may ensue to the rude and credulous populace: Therefore, partly imitating the example of well governed cities in Italy and many other nations... we will and command to be instituted a perpetual College of learned and grave men who shall publicly exercise medicine in our City of London and the suburbs, and within seven miles from that City on every side.*

Thus, the Italian Renaissance and its most eminent doctor (*'clarissimo medico'*) at the time, Thomas Linacre, conceived the Royal College of Physicians, a *collegio* that far outgrew its ancestors.

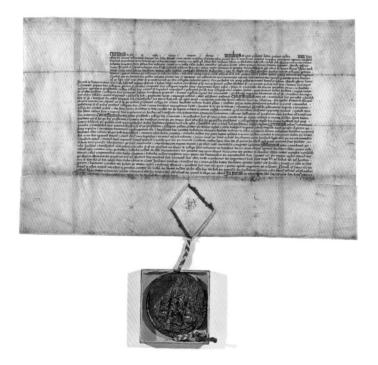

KILLYLEAGH, IRELAND AND KINGSTON, JAMAICA

KRISHNA CHINTHAPALLI

Sir Hans Sloane, painted by Thomas Murray c.1725
(© Royal College of Physicians)

Hans Sloane was born in Killyleagh, Ireland in 1660, and became a fellow of the Royal College of Physicians by the age of twenty-seven as well as President at the age of fifty-nine. From childhood, he was fascinated by plants and known to collect them from the seashore. Later, he went to France to study botany, as well as anatomy and medicine. He obtained his degree in physic with the highest honours and returned to England. Within three years, Sloane's interest in natural history led him to accept a post as personal physician to the new governor of Jamaica, in the Caribbean Sea.

After he arrived in Jamaica, Sloane successfully amassed and described hundreds of new animals and plants across the West Indies. Unfortunately, his time there was cut short by the death of the governor just over a year after they arrived. Even so, Sloane brought back the largest ever collection of new plants to England. During his excursions, he encountered the cocoa tree, introduced there from the Americas by the Spanish. Sloane was told that a cocoa drink was the local cure for indigestion, but described that the preparation was 'in great quantities, nauseous, and hard of digestion'.

Illustration of the cacao tree, depicted in Sloane's *Voyage to the Islands and Jamaica, Vol 2*. (© Royal College of Physicians)

Nonetheless, he brought back drawings and specimens of the plant and bean. Sloane also devised a recipe in which the beans were mixed with milk and sugar to make it more palatable as a remedy. This recipe for a milk chocolate drink may have been the first one used in England and became famous when it was bought and used by the Cadbury brothers in the following century.

Upon his second return to England, Sloane established himself in Great Russell Street as a meticulous physician who would also use new treatments, including chocolate. He treated royal figures including George II and his wife Caroline. Caroline had also instructed Sloane to study the Turkish practice of smallpox inoculation and provide it for her children. Sloane performed the inoculations, but only after it was tested on six prisoners condemned to death and six orphan children.

Sloane later published his research into the natural history of the Caribbean islands and the first new pharmacopoeia in London for over a century. For this work, he was rewarded by election to President of the Royal Society – the only time this post was held by a President of the Royal College of Physicians.

Throughout his life, he built up an enormous collection of manuscripts, artefacts, coins, gemstones, skeletons and, of course, plant specimens. When possible he also bought other people's collections and eventually had to buy the neighbouring house to store all of his items. Upon his death in 1753, he owned 50,000 books and 50,000 objects, and stipulated that they should be offered to the government, which bought them for £20,000. His collection formed the basis for the British Museum, located across the road from his house, and later, the Natural History Museum and the British Library.

However, back in Killyleagh, Sloane is remembered only for one discovery: an annual chocolate festival named after him.

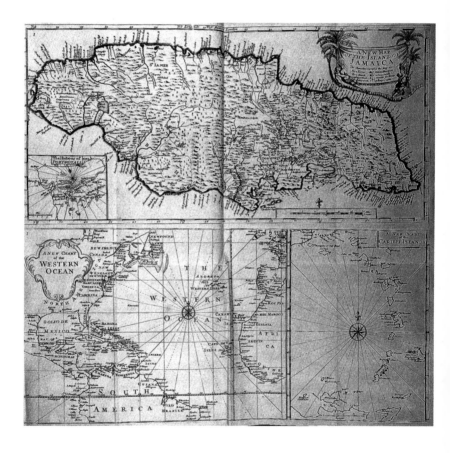

ABOVE: A pull-out plate from Vol 1 of Sloane's book, showing a new map of the island of Jamaica; a new chart of the Western Ocean, a new chart of the Caribee Islands. (Wellcome Collection)
OPPOSITE: The title page of Sloane's 1725 account of his journey to Jamaica (© Royal College of Physicians)

A

VOYAGE

To the ISLANDS

*Madera, Barbadoes, Nieves, S*ᵗ *Christophers,*

AND

JAMAICA;

WITH THE

Natural History

OF THE

Herbs and Trees, Four-footed Beasts, Fishes,
Birds, Insects, Reptiles, &c.

Of the last of those ISLANDS.

To which is prefix'd, An

INTRODUCTION,

Wherein is an ACCOUNT of the

Inhabitants, Air, Waters, Diseases, Trade, &c.

of that Place; with some Relations concerning the Neighbouring Continent, and Islands of *America.*

ILLUSTRATED WITH

The FIGURES of the Things described,

which have not been heretofore engraved.

𝔍𝔫 𝔩𝔞𝔯𝔤𝔢 𝔈𝔬𝔭𝔭𝔢𝔯-𝔓𝔩𝔞𝔱𝔢𝔰 𝔞𝔰 𝔟𝔦𝔤 𝔞𝔰 𝔱𝔥𝔢 𝔏𝔦𝔣𝔢.

By Sir *HANS SLOANE,* Barᵗ.

In Two Volumes.   Vol. II.

Many shall run to and fro, and Knowledge shall be increased. Dan. xii. 4.

LONDON:
Printed for the AUTHOR. 1725.

PHILADELPHIA, USA
KRISHNA CHINTHAPALLI

John Morgan (© University of Pennsylvania,
University Archives and Records Center)

'Why should we be deterred from establishing like institutions of Medicine in this seminary, especially as so many circumstances conspire to invite and encourage so important an undertaking?'

'Doctors are men who prescribe medicines of which they know little, to cure diseases of which they know less, in human beings of whom they know nothing,' said Voltaire, the French philosopher. No wonder that John Morgan, an American physician, came back to study in London in January 1765 after meeting Voltaire in Geneva. It would be a very remarkable year for Morgan.

Morgan grew up in Philadelphia and was in the first year of students who graduated from the College of Philadelphia in 1757. Being interested in medicine, he came to Europe to complete his training, with letters of recommendation from none other than Benjamin Franklin. Morgan gained his medical degree in Edinburgh and then re-trod a familiar route from London to Padua, stopping in France, the Netherlands and Switzerland.

Upon returning to London in 1765, he spent most of January studying for the three examinations of the Royal College of Physicians. He had successful vivas in *Physiologia*, *Pathologia* and *Therapeutice* and he was admitted as a licentiate of the RCP. Even more impressively, he was elected a fellow of the Royal Society, based on a single doctoral thesis on the origin of pus.

He returned to Philadelphia and, in May 1765, published his *Discourse upon the institution of medical schools in America*. Here he remarked how Scottish medical students in Leyden returned to set up a medical school in Edinburgh and asks the citizens of Philadelphia: 'Why should we be deterred from establishing like institutions of Medicine in this seminary, especially as so many circumstances conspire to invite and encourage so important an undertaking?'

There were indeed compelling circumstances. Philadelphia was the largest city in the thirteen American colonies and was centrally located between all of them. The city already had its own hospital, one of the oldest in North America, near the existing college. The college itself was thriving and offered languages and arts courses; Morgan believed the study of Latin and Greek to be 'very necessary' to a physician and thus a new medical school could benefit from the college. Most importantly, he thought of medical students not as fortunate as he was:

> *Some there are indeed, and not a few, who cannot by any means afford the expense of crossing the Atlantic, to prosecute their studies abroad. The proposed institution will therefore prove highly beneficial to every class of student in Medicine.*

Morgan successfully persuaded the city to set up the first medical school in North America by the autumn of 1765. A young man could enrol if he was proficient in Latin, mathematics and natural sciences. From his time in London, Morgan recognised the value of clinical teaching, such as the anatomy lectures offered by the surgeon William Hunter. He therefore introduced bedside teaching at the nearby hospital for the students. He himself taught them the theory and practice of physick. Over 250 years later, the University of Pennsylvania medical school receives more government research funding than Harvard or Yale. Morgan's school is a fitting rebuttal to Voltaire's quip.

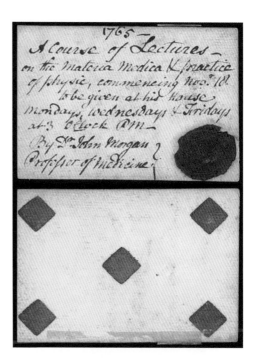

TOP: A ticket to Morgan's lecture series
ABOVE: The original medical school building in Philadelphia from an illustration in 1799. (Both images © University of Pennsylvania, University Archives and Records Center)

HUDSON BAY, CANADA AND MARRAKESH, MOROCCO

KRISHNA CHINTHAPALLI

He had criticised established physicians for neglecting to care for the poor, and gave free lectures to the public on the dangers of tobacco and alcohol use.

In 1836, Thomas Hodgkin was offered a fellowship by the Royal College of Physicians. He refused it. Hodgkin belonged to the Quakers, a denomination that split from the Anglican church, and he had a medical degree from Edinburgh. For over 300 years, the RCP had offered fellowships only to graduates of Oxford and Cambridge universities, and these universities offered study only to men who professed the Anglican faith. The RCP had repealed this requirement only two years before Hodgkin's invitation. However, Hodgkin believed he was only offered fellowship because he had established his reputation in pathology and that other deserving physicians would not be given the same opportunity.

As a medical student, he had moved to Paris for a year. Here he met René Laennec, the inventor of the stethoscope, and Baron von Humboldt, a famous explorer who sparked Hodgkin's interest in the peoples around the world. At the age of twenty-four, he was working at Guy's Hospital and gave a lecture on Laennec's stethoscope and how to use it. Deaf to his words, the hospital physicians turned the stethoscope upright and used it as a flowerpot. Fortunately, after they left, curious students experimented on each other with it. After promotion to Inspector of the Dead at Guy's Hospital, Hodgkin went on to provide the first descriptions of aortic regurgitation, appendicitis and, of course, lymphoma.

Hodgkin's decision to turn down fellowship may have contributed to Guy's Hospital in London refusing to offer him a post as physician, even though he had been a brilliant pathologist there for twelve years. However, it was not the only reason. He had criticised established physicians for neglecting to care for the poor, and gave free lectures to the public on the dangers of tobacco and alcohol use, as well as the need for bathing, exercise and sewage disposal. He also pushed for social reform in England and, at twenty-one,

ABOVE: René Laënnec treats a patient at the Necker Hospital, Paris. Heliogravure, after a painting, by Théobold Chartran. (Wellcome Collection)
LEFT: Nineteenth-century stethoscopes from the Symons collection (© Royal College of Physicians)
OPPOSITE: Thomas Hodgkin (Wellcome Collection)

he had already published an essay on humanitarian obligations that the British Empire owed to other races under its rule. He helped to found the University of London, the first secular university in England, and the Aborigines Protection Society. He called for the abolition of slavery and invited freed slaves to his home. They were asked to travel with him in an open carriage on the streets of London, as was Hesh-ton-a-quet, a tribal chief from Canada.

Hesh-ton-a-quet had been brought to London to be displayed publicly in the city. He was left destitute afterwards

and then, worse, imprisoned on spurious charges. Hodgkin put up the bail money and, after the chief's acquittal, drove him to Guy's Hospital to protest at his treatment to the hospital administrator, Benjamin 'King' Harrison. Harrison was a board member of the Hudson Bay Company, which made huge profits from trading furs for whisky with natives in Canada. For some European companies, plying native tribes with alcohol helped them increase their profits at the expense of destroying their way of life. Hodgkin believed Harrison would not be able to condone such actions, but he misjudged him. Harrison was a dictator who controlled every aspect of Guy's Hospital and when he stated that he would not let anyone who had been seen with a native American to work in the hospital, it was the end of Hodgkin's career and his contribution to scientific medicine.

Hodgkin could still have practised privately as a licentiate of the RCP, but he never liked collecting fees from patients. In fact, friends would avoid consulting him because they knew he would not accept their money. His practice declined and he occupied himself in philanthropic adventures with a Jewish banker, Sir Moses Montefiore.

At the age of sixty-five, Hodgkin and Montefiore heard about the unjust imprisonment, torture and execution of Jewish suspects of a murder in Morocco. Within two weeks, they had set off for the country after asking the British ambassador there to plead with the Moroccan government to halt further executions. In Tangier, they secured the release of both Jewish and Moorish prisoners imprisoned without trial. They then travelled towards Marrakesh, the capital. Upon arrival, as Hodgkin saw patients including the Prime Minister, Montefiore obtained an edict promising equal rights for Jewish citizens.

On another mission to Egypt and Palestine to build a hospital, Hodgkin developed intractable dysentery and realised he was dying. In his last letter to his wife, he wrote 'My dear love to all my friends. I lament the little service I have done.'

Thomas Hodgkin suffered from not accepting the fellowship, but the RCP suffered more without Hodgkin's noble and visionary ideas. One hopes that Hodgkin would be proud to be a fellow of the current RCP.

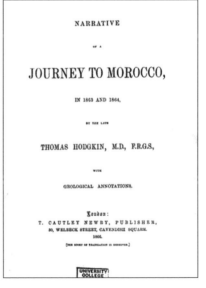

NARRATIVE

of a

JOURNEY TO MOROCCO,

IN 1863 AND 1864,

BY THE LATE

THOMAS HODGKIN, M.D., F.R.G.S,

WITH

GEOLOGICAL ANNOTATIONS.

London:

T. CAUTLEY NEWBY, PUBLISHER,
30, WELBECK STREET, CAVENDISH SQUARE.
1866.

[THE RIGHT OF TRANSLATION IS RESERVED.]

UNIVERSITY
COLLEGE

TOP: Mandingo prayer sheet presented to Thomas Hodgkin by the first president of Liberia (Wellcome Collection)
ABOVE: Title page of Hodgkin's Journey to Morocco (Wellcome Collection)
OPPOSITE: Native Americans at a Hudson Bay trading centre post (Stock Montage/Getty Images)

FORMOSA AND AMOY, CHINA

KRISHNA CHINTHAPALLI

During the spring of 1875, Patrick Manson was on holiday in London. He spent most of it in the reading room of the world's largest library, the British Museum library, encountering Karl Marx, among others. But his most memorable experience was of reading about the recent discovery of tiny worms in the blood of an Indian patient.

Manson was a customs doctor in Formosa (Taiwan) and then Amoy (Xiamen). His official duty was to inspect and treat sailors arriving into the harbour. He would also treat the local population for common conditions, such as elephantiasis. In one year alone, he had removed one ton of elephantoid tissue from patients. Manson realised that his patients had similar symptoms to the reported Indian patient and he returned from London to Amoy armed with a microscope. With his new instrument, he examined the blood of his patients and found similar worms trapped in a transparent sheath at an apparently embryonic stage. One such patient was his own gardener, Hin Lo.

Hin Lo was persuaded to stay in a room in Manson's house and have blood taken every three hours for two weeks. Manson was puzzled by what he found. The embryonic worms were present in blood only at around midnight each day. He noticed that the worm sheaths could

be made to rupture by cooling the blood with ice. He wondered if a hidden adult worm in the body was releasing worm embryos into the blood and if these embryos were seeking out a cooler environment in which to 'hatch'. His ingenious idea was that a cold-blooded insect could ingest the embryos, which would then grow up in its new host.

After musing on fleas and lice, Manson decided that mosquitoes were most likely, given their nocturnal feeding habits. Nothing was then known about mosquitoes, and he could find no information on them. Even the British Museum library apologised for not having any books on mosquitoes, but sent him a book on cockroaches, hoping it would suffice.

Mosquito illustration from Manson's Tropical Diseases (Wellcome Collection)

Patrick Manson (Wellcome Collection)

Sun Yat-Sen (Public domain)

Thus, his hapless gardener was transferred to a hut covered in fine gauze with one door. The hut was lit and the door was opened each night to let mosquitoes in, before trapping them inside after thirty minutes. In the morning, Manson incapacitated the engorged mosquitoes with tobacco smoke and dissected them. The worms were present throughout and he could see their stages of growth from embryos in the mosquito stomach to juvenile worms in the thorax muscles. Manson had discovered the first disease to be transmitted between humans by insects.

When his findings on filariasis and transmission were presented at a meeting in London, there was heckling and one critic remarked that while it could be the work of a genius, it was more likely to be the 'the emanations of a drunken Scots doctor in far-off China'.

Six years after presenting his research, Manson moved to Hong Kong and founded the first medical school there. He also saw that children were undernourished, partly because milk was scarce and too expensive for most inhabitants. Thus he set up a dairy farm, with farmers and cows arriving there from his home in Aberdeenshire.

One day in 1896, Manson, who had returned to London, and a colleague, James Cantlie, received a hand-delivered note from one of their former medical students in Hong Kong. It read: 'I was kidnapped into the Chinese Legation on Sunday and shall be smuggled out from England to China for death. Pray, rescue me quick.'

This physician had been in solitary confinement for six days but finally convinced his guard to deliver the note with the promise of money, after building a relationship with him over their shared socialist ideology. Over that weekend, Manson and Cantlie stationed themselves all night outside the Legation after hearing that the physician would be smuggled out in a barrel and then thrown overboard into the Thames. On Monday, they alerted the press and the Foreign Office, forcing the Legation to release their captive to great publicity. That doctor, Sun Yat-Sen, returned to overthrow the imperial dynasty in China and become the country's first president.

Manson's most important contributions to medicine were still to come though. He secured funding for a surgeon, Ronald Ross, to travel with the army to India and study malaria. He then mentored Ross during his years of research there. When Ross showed that mosquitoes also transmitted malaria, his essay concluded: 'These observations prove the mosquito theory of malaria as expounded by Dr Patrick Manson and, in conclusion, I should add that I have constantly received the benefit of his advice during the enquiry.'

The London medical community was no more ready to accept the mosquito theory of malaria than it was for filariasis, which he had discovered in Amoy. Manson therefore arranged an experiment in which mosquitoes that had fed on patients with benign malaria were shipped to London. The mosquitoes were then applied to the hand of Manson's son, a medical student. He developed malaria two weeks later with parasites present in his blood film.

Thereby Manson had shown the world the link between mosquitoes and malaria, a disease that has killed billions of people throughout history. He also showed exactly how those tiny worms, which he had read about years earlier, had made their way into the human bloodstream.

Patrick Manson experimenting with *filaria sanguinis* on his gardener (Wellcome Collection)

VIENNA, AUSTRIA
KRISHNA CHINTHAPALLI

'If girls were encouraged to use their brains the excitement caused thereby would produce insanity,' said one member of the RCP in 1878 of its decision to refuse admission to women. It took over thirty more years before women could become members, and even then it was with the persuasion of the Royal College of Surgeons, which had already opened its membership to women.

The expansion of membership occurred at the time that Helen Mackay enrolled to study at the Royal Free School of Medicine for Women. Shortly after the First World War (1914–18) and the corresponding shortage of male physicians, she became the first woman consultant at a London hospital other than the Royal Free. Mackay had secured a post in Queen's Hospital, Hackney, in the East End of London, but soon interrupted her work there to go to Vienna.

Helen Mackay (© Royal College of Physicians)

Vienna was a starving city during the First World War. Within a year of the start of hostilities, the capital of Austria-Hungary had issued ration cards for flour and bread to its citizens, followed by rationing of milk, sugar and butter in 1916. The city had been highly dependent on food imports and could not feed its population following the Russian invasion of farmlands in its eastern empire, the Allied naval blockade in the Mediterranean Sea and the drop in food imports from Hungary. By 1919, Viennese physicians estimated that 10 per cent of the city's population were dying directly from starvation.

Mackay travelled to Vienna in 1920 as part of a British research team to conduct a trial of cod liver oil in infants to prevent rickets, which was

'If girls were encouraged to use their brains the excitement caused thereby would produce insanity,' said one member of the RCP in 1878 of its decision to refuse admission to women.

widespread there. During the study, the team had also discovered that their results varied greatly between winter and summer. They realised that direct sunshine (unfiltered by glass) or cod liver oil could prevent the onset of rickets.

Most of the same infants were also anaemic, which was not a surprise as physicians knew that both conditions often co-existed and may have the same cause. However, Mackay went on to study the prevalence and severity of anaemia in childhood. Anaemia was difficult to measure as it does not affect the red blood cell count, which was commonly used to diagnose anaemia, but causes smaller red blood cells to develop with less haemoglobin. Mackay had calculated normal values for haemoglobin levels and found that it was low in children. She also realised that anaemia was not cured using treatments for rickets.

Mackay returned to Hackney and continued investigations over the following decade. She found that haemoglobin levels fall slowly from birth, especially in non-breastfed infants. Further studies showed that the reason was iron deficiency, and that iron supplementation prevented anaemia, increased weight and halved the rate of infections in the group of children she studied.

As a result of her discoveries, Mackay was the first woman to be admitted as a fellow of the RCP in 1934 and this was one of many honours she received. The excitement of her honour did not lead to insanity and perhaps this encouraged the RCP to appoint more women fellows, albeit reluctantly.

Seven years after Mackay's election, the then President of the RCP announced, without irony, at the Royal Free School of Medicine's graduation ceremony, that 'medical women make excellent wives, while their qualification is always a second string to their bow'.

Finally, in this century, there is parity: the RCP has elected a female President as many times as it has elected a male President (as of 2018).

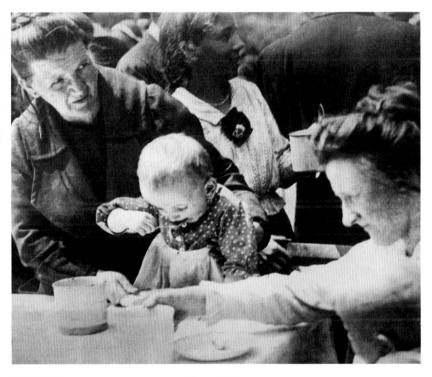

OPPOSITE: Unemployed men on the streets of Vienna, 1920
ABOVE: Mothers feeding their children at a food relief station after the end of the First World War (both images © Bettman/Getty Images)

THE WORLD IN 2018
KRISHNA CHINTHAPALLI

In contrast to the other books in this series, this final volume focuses on the present and future of medicine around the world. Physicians from the RCP have kindly offered an insight into some of the exceptional work that they do. They are those from both the UK and those working abroad. Some are just starting their careers, while others are already internationally renowned.

Providing care to those who are in need is at the heart of a physician's duty. **Aula Abbara** travels to refugee camps for displaced Syrian people in Greece and Turkey. **David Martin** flies to Bolivia to treat the cardiac complications of Chagas disease and **Gail Davey** journeys to Ethiopia, where she has led the effort to treat podoconiosis, a much-neglected tropical disease. During a recent Ebola virus outbreak in Sierra Leone, **Colin Brown** helped to provide urgent care. **Peter Goulden** provides care to an under-served community of Marshall Islanders in southern USA, who were displaced by atomic bomb testing.

In the forests of Chhattisgarh, India, **Ed Armstrong** helped to treat people with multi-drug-resistant tuberculosis and this is an area intensively studied by **Zarir Udwadia** in the concrete jungle of Mumbai. In nearby Malaysia, **Yook Chin Chia** is helping to raise awareness of one of the leading causes of renal disease: high blood pressure. **Maisam Akroush**, the first female gastroenterologist in Jordan, is similarly helping those with chronic liver disease overcome stigma and barriers to care. **Thofique Adamjee** gives an account of healthcare information technology advances in Singapore.

Doctors are also present at the extreme ends of the world, studying or treating patients. **Roger Thompson** has travelled up mountains in Bolivia to analyse the body's response to high altitudes, whereas **Carl Edmonds** explored the depths of the Pacific Ocean to advance diving medicine. **Richard Corbett** provided care for people in a setting that could be more inaccessible than space: the frozen wilderness of Antarctica. In a different desert in Afghanistan, **Damian Jenkins** was a military doctor amid the hostility of war.

Educating the next generation of doctors is a role the RCP takes very seriously; **Nigel and Deborah Bax** explain how they are helping with this in post-war Iraq. In Iceland, **Tomas Agustsson** is using the RCP's help to implement a new system of training for postgraduate physicians, and in Africa **Evarist Njelesani** received support in setting up the East, Central and Southern Africa College of Physicians. In Yangon General Hospital, Myanmar, **Thet Naung** studies for membership of the RCP and to take part in an RCP training scheme for international doctors.

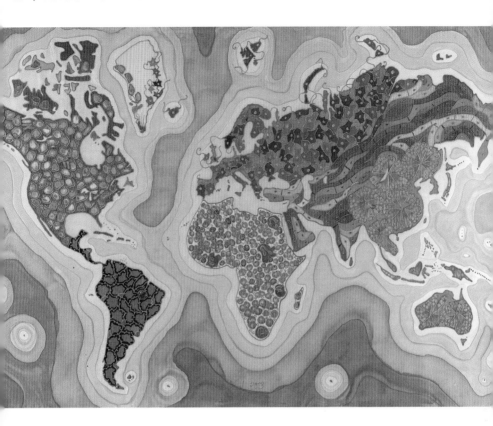

Finally, we have brave physicians who have investigated the harms from our own products. **Javed Akram** investigated a new syndrome in Pakistan, eventually tracing it back to drug contamination. **Judith Mackay** in Hong Kong has spent most of her life standing up to the tobacco industry and exposing the harm it does, even though she has faced death threats and was named one of the three most dangerous people in the world by the industry.

These people are a tiny fraction of the 34,000 members and fellows of the Royal College of Physicians, 6,000 of whom work internationally, in more than 110 countries.

ABOVE: A map of the world by doctor and artist Odra Noel. Each area of the map is made up of human tissue relating to the main health problems within those areas. Adipose tissue represents obesity in North America; lung tissue represents smoking in Central and South America; neurons represent neurodegeneration in Europe; cardiac muscle represents hypertension and heart failure in the Middle East and Central Asia; pancreatic acinar tissue represents diabetes in the Far East and Pacific; blood represents transmissible infections in Africa

AFRICA

ETHIOPIA, SIERRA LEONE, KENYA, LESOTHO, MALAWI, MAURITIUS, SWAZILAND, TANZANIA, UGANDA, ZAMBIA, ZIMBABWE

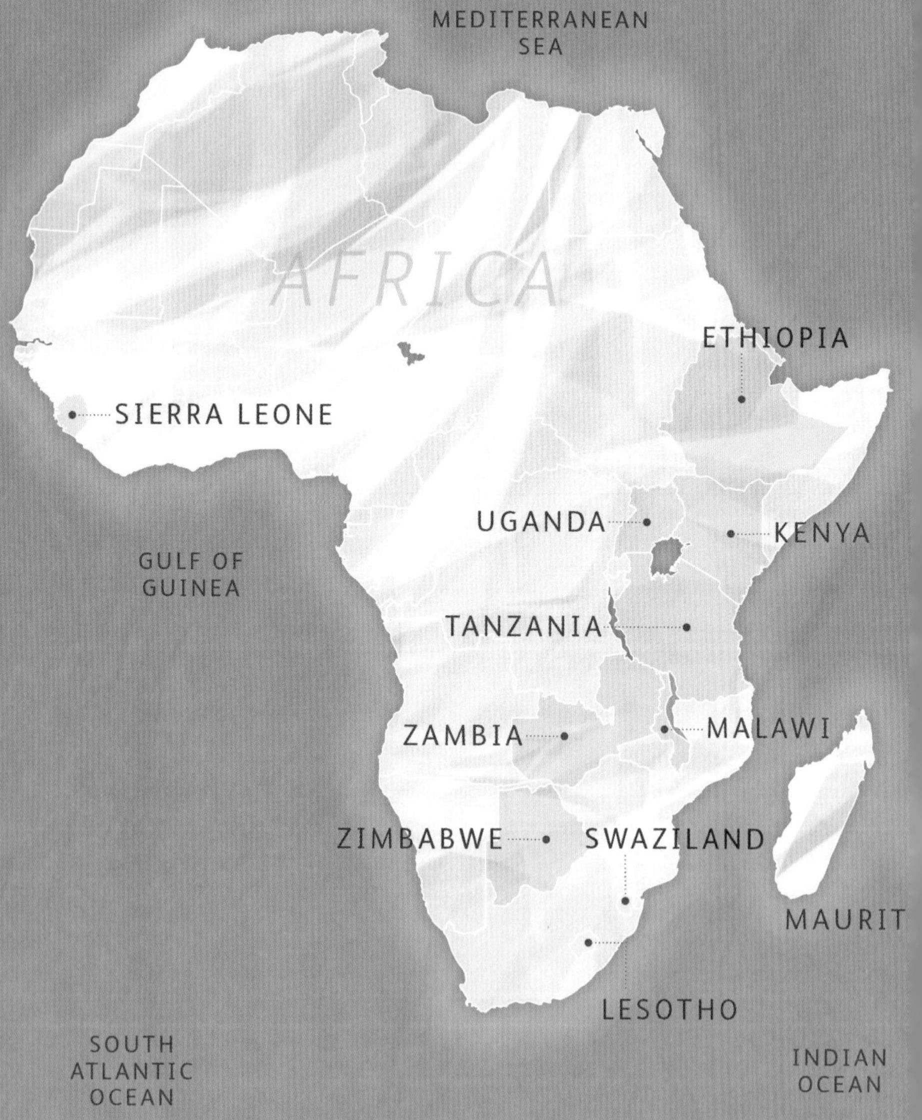

MEDITERRANEAN SEA

AFRICA

ETHIOPIA

SIERRA LEONE

GULF OF GUINEA

UGANDA

KENYA

TANZANIA

ZAMBIA

MALAWI

ZIMBABWE

SWAZILAND

MAURIT

LESOTHO

SOUTH ATLANTIC OCEAN

INDIAN OCEAN

SIERRA LEONE AND THE EBOLA VIRUS

DR COLIN BROWN MRCP

The 2014–16 West African Ebola Virus Disease (EVD) outbreak has forever changed the way the world will look at epidemic preparedness. As Infectious Diseases Advisor for the King's Sierra Leone Partnership (KSLP), a development organisation based in Freetown, the capital city of Sierra Leone, I saw first-hand the devastation the disease brought, through working in partnership with Connaught Hospital, the only adult medical referral facility in the country.

I spent nearly six months in the country during the epidemic. I started there during the early planning stages when the Western Area, a peninsula containing Freetown, was mainly unaffected and the disease was limited to rural, eastern provinces. We worked in tandem with the Ministry of Health and Sanitation to prepare Freetown hospitals for the arrival of the first cases including staff training in infection prevention and control, and safe isolation of cases. Later, in the peak period of transmission, we regularly had more patients than EVD Holding Unit beds. Every day, we would have to decide who to admit into our unit, often choosing between the sickest (also the most infectious) and the youngest, often tragically orphaned by the disease. Finally, during the epidemic tail, we were able to trial rapid diagnostic tests and improve algorithms for disease detection to improve management.

ABOVE: The Ebola Holding Unit at the Connaught Hospital, where the nursing staff have left the ward and are heading to decontaminate (© Michael Duff/KSLP)

OVERLEAF CLOCKWISE FROM TOP LEFT: The initial entry doors to the Ebola Holding Unit – these changed significantly over time to become one way opaque spring loaded doors (© Joanna Dunlop). Nursing staff in full Personal Protective Equipment ready to enter the Ebola Holding Unit (© Simon Davis/DFID). Early Ministry of Health & Sanitation/ UNICEF poster warning of the signs and symptoms of Ebola Virus Disease (© Simon Davis/DFID)

ISOLATION
ROOM

NO
ENTRY

EBOLA

unicef

Signs and Symptoms

FEVER

BLEEDING

BLOODY DIARRHOEA

HEALTH
CENTRE

SKIN RASH

VOMITING BLOOD

MUSCLE OR JOINT PAIN

**If you have Fever, Diarrhoea and Vomiting with or without Bleeding
GO IMMEDIATELY TO THE NEAREST HEALTH FACILITY**

For more information call 117 (Toll Free)

EBOLA KEY MESSAGES unic

What is Ebola ?

Ebola is a killer disease caused by a virus. It spreads quickly from person to person, kills in a
time BUT can be prevented.

Signs & Symptoms

FEVER VOMITING BLOODY BLEEDING MUSCLE OR
BLOOD DIARRHOEA JOINT PAIN

How is Ebola Spread?

It is spread through:

- Direct contact with wounds, body fluids like blood, saliva, vomitus, stool, urine of an infected person
  or splashing of such fluids from an infected person to another person and un-sterilized injections.
- Using skin piercing instruments that have been used by an infected person.
- Direct physical handling of persons who have died of Ebola.
- Eating bush meats especially monkeys, chimpanzees, bats and dead animals.
- Eating fruits that bats or wild animals have partly eaten (bat mot).

How can Ebola be Prevented?

Persons suspected to be Persons suspected to have Wash hands with
suffering from Ebola died of Ebola must be reported soap after touching
should be referred to immediately to a health worker. a sick person.
the nearest health facility Avoid washing the body
immediately. and bury immediately.

Do not share sharp Avoid eating bush meat Avoid eating fruits that
objects such as needle, especially Monkeys, bats or wild animals have
razor blades, etc. Chimpanzees and Bats. partly eaten (Bat Mot)

For More Information Call FREE 117

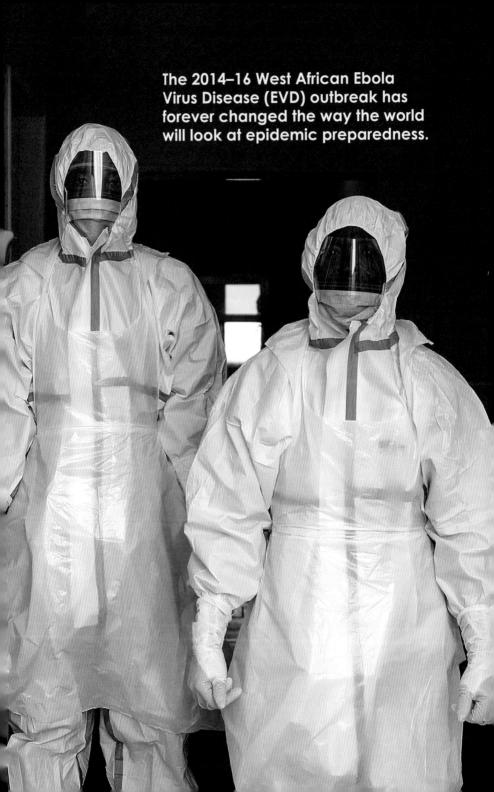

The 2014–16 West African Ebola Virus Disease (EVD) outbreak has forever changed the way the world will look at epidemic preparedness.

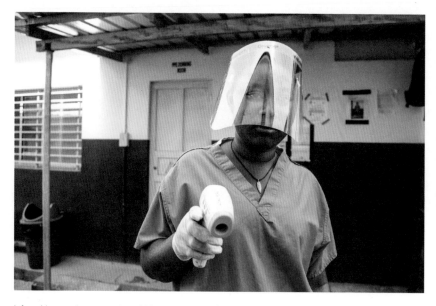

Infrared temperature screening, which every patient, relative, visitor and member of staff had taken on entry to Connaught Hospital (© Simon Davis/DFID)

The challenges that the hospital, the region and the country faced were exceptional – there is a population of six million people and only 136 doctors in total to face the EVD challenge. Through the bravery of the local medical, nursing, cleaning and allied healthcare staff who manned the units, with help from international volunteers and coordination and support from donor agencies, Sierra Leone is now better placed to face future infectious disease threats, such as cholera. The country now has disease control mechanisms that can be rapidly recalled, newly developed expertise in command and control structures, EVD case management experience, and a programmatic organisation of outbreak response.

Personally, I find Salone, as Sierra Leone is known locally, an incredible country. It has emerged from over a decade of civil war with resilience and charm, only to face one of the gravest public health and humanitarian threats of the century. I first became involved with KSLP thanks to Oliver Johnson, our programme director, who set up the partnership based on his elective experience as a medical student. I first visited Sierra Leone in 2013, and as with the KSLP vision, very much hope to be involved in developing services and care there for the foreseeable future. The medical environment in Freetown is very challenging, with limited physical and human resources, as well as limited radiological and laboratory diagnostic tests. It was a pleasure watching RCP fellow Dr Terry Gibson take on a major leadership role in training the junior medical staff during the EVD epidemic, relaying his decades of medical experience and enduring what seemed like unending ward rounds of Connaught Hospital. He has inspired many young doctors, both Sierra

Leonean and British volunteers, to progress in their training as physicians. One point that is immediately apparent on visiting is the invaluable breadth of resources and training opportunities we have available to us in the UK: dedicated postgraduate training in medical specialties, healthcare free at the point of access to all, and ease of access to diagnostic tests that we often take for granted. Despite the lack of facilities, it is an exciting experience for a young doctor and a real opportunity to learn how to think on your feet and work with limited resources. Our dedicated Salone colleagues, who manage with what they have available to them, must train in other countries to become specialists, must diagnose and treat severely ill patients with few investigations, and must fit this around what patients can afford. Because of them, Sierra Leone responded to the virus outbreak in a manner that belies its small size and limited resources.

ABOVE: Dr Brown in scrubs after exiting a shift in the Ebola Holding Unit (© Michael Duff/KSLP)
BELOW: An ambulance being directed towards the Ebola Holding Unit (© Joanna Dunlop)

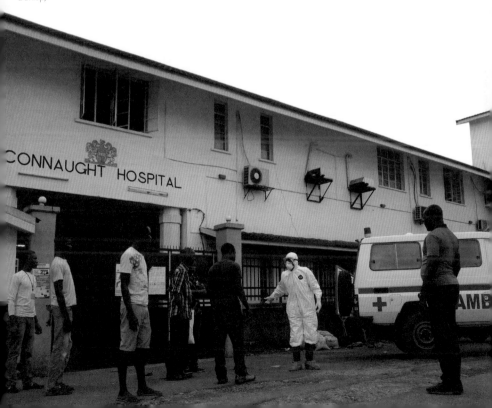

EAST, CENTRAL AND SOUTHERN AFRICA COLLEGE OF PHYSICIANS:

KENYA, LESOTHO, MALAWI, MAURITIUS, SWAZILAND, TANZANIA, UGANDA, ZAMBIA AND ZIMBABWE

PROFESSOR EVARIST NJELESANI FCP (ECSA) FRCP

The East, Central and Southern Africa Health Community comprises nine countries and is home to more than 200 million people. There is a documented lack of access to well-trained physicians in the region: the latest World Health Organization figures show that the physician-to-population ratio does not exceed 20 per 100,000 anywhere in the region, and may be as low as 2 per 100,000 in some countries. This compares to 280 per 100,000 in the UK.

Current output from the region's existing postgraduate programmes is simply not sufficient to match demand. It is estimated that it would take over a century to reach a target of 50 physicians per 100,000 population. I first met with colleagues from six countries in Nairobi in 2012 to consider a new association of physicians across our borders. Initially, we were all keen to coordinate postgraduate training programmes for physicians, because each country had different standards. This developed into discussions for a college.

Right from the word go, the energy in the group was infectious and we were determined to make this happen. We had discussions around a common curriculum and implementation under regional supervision. Therefore, we set out to develop a constitution, a strategic plan and a resource mobilisation plan.

Doctors in Moi, Kenya (© Medical Images)

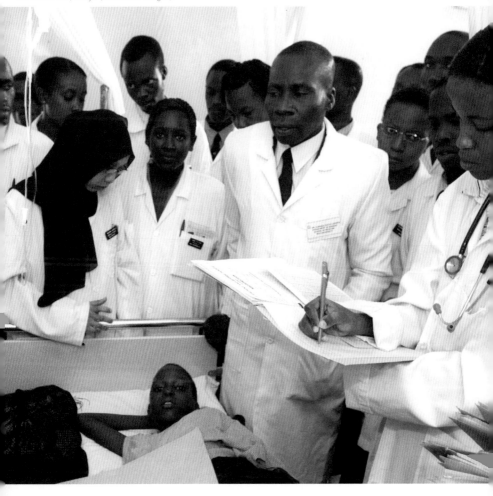

The biggest challenge would be to have all our stakeholders on board, a lesson learned from our sister College of Surgeons. We invited our sister college as well as higher education authorities, health ministers, medical schools, senior physicians, public service commissions and faith-based organisations involved in rural health services. During this formative stage, the RCP was a key partner and provided support from senior physicians and officers, who were instrumental in developing our constitution and strategy. This collaboration has been fantastic and I anticipate it to go from strength to strength. Eventually, East, Central and Southern African Health Ministers approved the establishment of the College at their annual meeting in Mauritius in December 2015. Our mission was to improve standards of healthcare throughout the region by providing specialist training of physicians committed to lifelong learning.

On 1 July 2016, the East, Central and Southern Africa College Of Physicians (ECSACOP) was inaugurated by Ministers of Health from Zambia and Zimbabwe. We held a colourful ceremony in Victoria Falls, Zimbabwe, and we invited all those who had supported us, including the RCP, the College of Surgeons, the West African College of Physicians and the College of Physicians in South Africa. Retired physicians were also among our guests, including the first African cardiologist. We also conferred Foundation Fellowship on 200 physicians from member countries during the ceremony.

ECSACOP has four aims: firstly, we will work in partnership with governments, universities and healthcare providers to expand and improve postgraduate training and provision of quality healthcare. Secondly, we will be a voice for the patient and the profession, recognised as a regional leader in advocating for healthcare improvement and disease prevention. Thirdly, we will support physicians' lifelong learning and career development. And fourthly, we will establish an internationally recognised and financially sustainable college. By engaging with our national associations of physicians, examinations will be jointly developed, within a jointly developed curriculum framework.

At the moment, we are a virtual college, but we aim to have a small secretariat in each country along with two training centres. We will establish these training centres primarily in hospitals that serve rural populations, in an attempt to reduce disparities in access and standards of care between urban and rural areas. We are currently working on accreditation criteria for training centres and for future trainers.

Going back to the shortage of physicians, ECSACOP's new postgraduate medical qualifications will aim to be internationally recognised and so help to supplement the number of physicians who are currently being trained. Our College will offer membership to physicians after two years of training and then fellowship at the end of training. This will also remove different standards between countries. The College is determined to make a positive impact on the health status of communities in East, Central and Southern Africa.

ETHIOPIA AND PODOCONIOSIS

PROFESSOR GAIL DAVEY MRCP

After my doctorate in London, I was keen to work abroad in epidemiology and Ethiopia offered an unmissable opportunity. One of my mentors had mentioned there was a post available as an assistant professor in the Department of Community Health in Addis Ababa. At the same time, my husband had just retired as an international long-distance runner but was offered the chance to help organise a regular running event in Ethiopia (he became co-founder and general manager of the Great Ethiopian Run). We had planned to move there for two years but stayed for ten. We loved the people and the culture. Ethiopia has never been colonised and has an enormous hunger for knowledge and progress.

Soon after our move, the British ambassador asked me to review a grant application to the British Embassy by a small charity in a remote part of Ethiopia. The grant was for a condition called podoconiosis, for which there was very little existing research. Even some of my colleagues in Addis Ababa had not heard of it, so I assumed it was a very rare disease. I travelled out to Wolayita zone to assess the project and realised

Barefoot life in northern Ethiopia (© Roberto Fumagalli/Alamy)

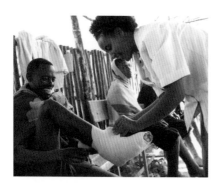 

LEFT: A patient receives treatment for podoconiosis (© Jake Lyell/Alamy)
RIGHT: Patient learning to use bandages (© Gail Davey)

that podoconiosis was actually a very common disease in this part of the country.

In fact, podoconiosis has a nationwide prevalence of 4 per cent in people aged 15 years or older from our own survey in 2013. It was just under-recognised in Ethiopia and internationally. When talking to a room full of public health doctors, I would sometimes put up a photo of the condition and ask about it. Most of them would agree that they had seen it but did not know a term for it or thought it was lymphatic filariasis, which is another cause of elephantiasis, caused by filarial parasites. This may be because podoconiosis is a disease of people who live in very remote areas who are poor and therefore have no voice. Many of the locals also think it is due to a curse or evil magic and not physical causes. The disease is unlikely to affect tourists or soldiers, and so there is less impetus to treat from a strategic or economic viewpoint.

Podoconiosis was first recognised as a distinct disease in the 1970s. Ernest Price, a leprosy specialist in Addis Ababa, saw patients referred to him for foot swelling and discovered that their disease was due to direct foot contact with volcanic red clay soil. He named it after the Greek words for foot (*podos*) and dust (*konos*). Constant exposure to the soil causes absorption of irritant particles into the lymph nodes and lymph vessels, which become blocked, thus causing progressive irreversible swelling of the feet and legs.

When I realised that there was no routine care provision for almost any of these people with podoconiosis, I was keen to combine research with policy change, advocacy and treatment right from the start. Sometimes, good quality research is not sufficient by itself and, because podoconiosis was not on anybody else's radar, I thought advocacy was needed. During the time I was living in Ethiopia, it was harder to raise international awareness. However, in 2010, after moving to Brighton, it became much easier to explain the situation – I gave a lunchtime seminar to the Neglected Tropical Diseases department at the World Health Organization (WHO) headquarters in Geneva. They quickly realised that it was a serious health issue and that treatment for lymphatic filariasis would also treat people suffering from podoconiosis. In 2012, podoconiosis appeared for the first time as a Neglected Tropical Disease on the WHO website.

Treatment of podoconiosis is based on reducing contact with the soil. For example, footwear and regular foot washing help prevent the disease. In 2012, I set up Footwork, the International Podoconiosis Initiative, to help provide an international response to podoconiosis and have been lucky to be supported by a number of other individuals and organisations, including a shoe manufacturer. Hundreds of thousands of shoes have been distributed in Ethiopia, not just through podoconiosis projects, but also in schools and orphanages. The Ethiopian government and partners have trained hundreds of health workers to manage podoconiosis and raise awareness.

There are large numbers of affected people who will not be cured now but we aim to prevent new cases, especially in young people. With continued funding and advocacy, I hope to see the elimination of the disease within our lifetimes.

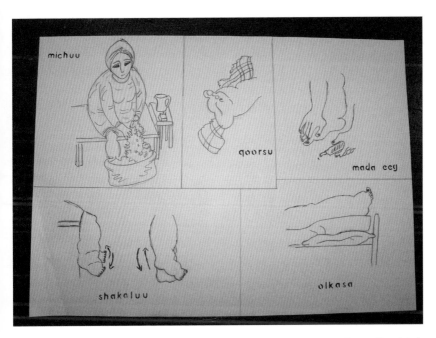

Information for patients in the Afaan Oromo language (© Nina Janssen-Fedoroff/Wollega Ethiopia Foundation)

EUROPE

ICELAND, GREECE, SYRIA, JORDAN

ICELAND

NORWEGIAN
SEA

NORTH
SEA

EUROPE

MEDITERRANEAN
SEA

GREECE

BLACK
SEA

SYRIA

JORD

CORE MEDICAL TRAINING IN ICELAND

DR TOMAS AGUSTSSON FRCP

Our medical school in Iceland serves the world's smallest linguistic area, an island of 330,000 inhabitants who speak Icelandic. When I started medical school, we had thirty-six students per year. Most graduates will work at the University Hospital, Reykjavik, which has two sites and perhaps a surprisingly large number of specialties, including cardiothoracic surgery and neurosurgery. There are some services that we cannot sustain though, such as paediatric cardiac surgery, which is instead performed in the USA or Scandinavia. On the other hand, some doctors will work in health centres around the country, sometimes as the only doctor present, and will look after their population's basic healthcare needs.

Dr Agustsson (© Tomas Agustsson)

After finishing their first postgraduate year as a house officer, most of our doctors usually go abroad, especially to the USA or Scandinavia, to complete the rest of their specialty training. Those who stayed found that there was a limited structure to postgraduate training in Iceland. Hospital jobs or roles could be poorly defined and they had only a short training syllabus. Teaching was mostly didactic and given by the more enthusiastic members of staff.

I was one of few doctors who had decided to come to the UK. I was very impressed by doctors in Iceland who had trained in the UK; they had a broad base of medical knowledge and had a sensible way of doing things. It was difficult at first and I remember being frustrated by writing endless applications for jobs as a senior house officer until I secured a post in Oxford. I quickly

Core medical trainees at an introductory course held by the RCP's Education Department in Reykjavík. (© Tomas Agustsson)

found out that the workload was much greater than in Iceland and there was a more formal medical hierarchy. But I enjoyed the discipline of post-take ward rounds for new admissions each morning and clinical handovers at the end of my shift – these were often much more casual back home.

By the time I returned home to Landspitali Hospital in Reykjavik, I recognised that good training goes hand-in-hand with providing a good clinical service for our patients. As an example, we saw large fluctuations in the numbers of trainees, with almost no trainees in medicine in my hospital on one occasion, which of course affected patient care. Improving training could make local junior doctor jobs more attractive. At the same time, there was national legislation stating that all fully trained doctors must have completed a recognised training programme of some kind. Thus, there was a definite need to do more for trainees.

We looked at training programmes in North America and northern Europe. However, if you want to work in Iceland, then you must have a broad base in internal and acute medicine. For example, I am an endocrinologist and the bulk of my work here is in diabetes and internal medicine. We do not need specialists in Cushing's disease.

This generalist approach to medicine did not exist in many countries, such as in American residency programmes. I saw an opportunity to use my experience of the UK, and the other staff were interested in the core medical training curriculum used in the UK. The detail and the quality of the integrated curriculum as well as the online assessment system were better than others that we had seen. The way in which progress was recorded, the formal meetings with supervisors, the workplace-based assessments and the exams all provided a real measure of competence in different domains.

So we sent a simple query to the Joint Royal Colleges of Physicians Training Board (JRCPTB) asking if we could adapt the online portfolio system for UK doctors in core medical training. After further correspondence, we realised that we could develop our own core medical training programme with the help of the RCP. This then led to a visit by seven of our doctors and managers to London in November 2014. Here we explored all aspects of the UK's core medical training curriculum and assessments. RCP staff then visited Iceland regularly to train consultants in educational supervision and performing assessments of clinical skills.

A group of six of us then set about developing the programme and I was in charge of implementing the assessments and interacting with

Icebergs floating down from the Arctic Ocean towards Iceland (© Krishna Chinthapalli)

the JRCPTB, including its accreditation of our programme. However, the roles all became fluid and it was certainly a team effort in the end. In September 2015, we formally started our core medical training programme in the presence of the British ambassador and our government minister for health. By June 2016 it was assessed as being equivalent in standard to the UK core medical training programme: our trainees could now compete for specialty training in the UK after completion on an equal footing with UK doctors. Now we also hold the written MRCP exams in Iceland for the first time and our trainees had a pass rate of 71.4 per cent for Part 1 compared to 62 per cent in the UK – which we are very proud of!

Our collaboration has had huge repercussions for medicine in Iceland. Trainees now behave differently and are more up to date with medicine than we are because they are studying for examinations. Other specialties have been very impressed by our reforms. Anaesthetists, gynaecologists, psychiatrists and emergency medicine consultants have all started to form links with the relevant UK colleges to develop similar training programmes. The standard of training has been raised already and we will continue to build upon our success.

THE SYRIAN CIVIL WAR: GREECE, SYRIA AND THE ZA'ATARI REFUGEE CAMP, JORDAN

DR AULA ABBARA MRCP, INFECTIOUS DISEASES SPECIALTY TRAINEE

The bloody conflict in my home country, Syria, began in March 2011. Since then, half a million people have been killed and another million injured. More than half of the country's population is in need of assistance and there are over four million refugees. Most of these citizens now shelter in countries neighbouring Syria, in one of the worst refugee crises of the modern era.

For the last few years, I have worked with Hand in Hand for Syria (HIH), a UK charity that provides medical and humanitarian aid inside Syria, and the Syrian American Medical Society (SAMS). In 2013, I took one year out of my infectious diseases registrar training programme to work full time in Turkey and Jordan. In Jordan, I worked in primary care in the Za'atari camp in the north of the country and as an infectious diseases consult for complex bone, joint or neurosurgical infections. I also worked in a specialist surgical hospital with highly skilled Syrian doctors, who were themselves refugees in Jordan.

Teaching and training have been an important aspect of work. This included infectious diseases teaching in Jordan and also as part of acute care and intensive care training of Syrian health workers in eastern Turkey. This has been vital given that more than 700 health workers have been killed in the conflict and many more have left the country as they and their families have become targets. The result is that junior or non-medical staff take the place of physicians and surgeons, and also take on additional roles.

Hundreds of thousands of Syrians have also made the dangerous journey over land and sea to Europe. In 2016, SAMS invited me to join the steering committee of their new team to coordinate care of refugees in Greece. Our first medical volunteers and translators began working in informal refugee camps. In June 2016, these informal camps were cleared away with refugees transferred to Greek Ministry of Health camps. There are about twenty-nine camps

OPPOSITE: A boy plays in a refugee centre (© Abdulazez Dukhan)

Dr Abbara (© Aula Abbara)

A girl in a refugee centre (© Abdulazez Dukhan)

in northern Greece and they shelter a total of about 55,000 refugees. Once refugees reach the official camps, there is little indication to them of the next step or of how long they will be there.

We were requested by the United Nations High Commissioner for Refugees and the Greek Ministry of Health to manage healthcare in four official camps, alongside a humanitarian agency in each camp. The main work is primary healthcare. About half of the consultations are in paediatrics, and other illnesses include both infectious and non-communicable disease. Obstetric, gynaecological and psychological care is also in demand.

The project grew rapidly in capacity, infrastructure and professionalism in the first four months of its existence. We now have a core staff of ten people, including long-term medical and field coordinators based in Greece. In the first four

months of the project, we have had 140 volunteers, one-third of whom have been British, including senior consultants in the NHS. This has allowed us to develop protocols, triage and review systems for patients with chronic conditions or those who need antenatal care.

One treatment, which we are rapidly developing, is our psychosocial programme for refugees. Many refugees have experienced severe trauma in Syria, when travelling to Europe and even when in Europe, given their current living circumstances. One such initiative is being run by a British-Syrian psychologist in collaboration with the Children and War Foundation to build resilience in children and identify those who require more specialised psychological care. She teaches refugee volunteers, who will then, in turn, implement this programme with children over a six-week cycle.

Working with the refugees gives vital insights into their experiences, hardships and hopes. Many have suddenly and cruelly lost everything they had built up during their lives.

Life in the refugee camps (© Abdulazez Dukhan)

Working with the refugees gives vital insights into their experiences, hardships and hopes. Many have suddenly and cruelly lost everything they had built up during their lives. There are, of course, many stories which resonated with me. I met one man in Greece, of a similar age to my father. He had worked as an engineer in Syria and in some European countries during his career. With tears in his eyes, he talked about his home and his family, and how he had looked forward to enjoying his retirement. But that was shattered. He was now a refugee, not wanted in the European countries he had worked in. He had no home, no family with him and no future that he could imagine for himself. For all of the refugees, each day is the same as the last but compounded by uncertainty and with little control of either their own or their family's destiny. There is also the stark knowledge that they are seen as just another number. Encouraging international volunteers to work in our project reminds both volunteers and refugees of their common humanity rather than highlighting the differences.

I have so far found the experiences very challenging, yet rewarding. It has been a steep learning curve in understanding how to set up and manage clinics with the different stakeholders and legal regulations involved. This includes managing human resources – perhaps the most challenging but also the most important. It also means learning quickly about equipment hire, finance budgets and funding applications as well as then reporting to our funders.

The most striking characteristic of the project in Greece has been the compassion, dedication and hard work shown by the staff and volunteers. This has translated into culturally appropriate care of as high a standard as possible for the refugees, whose lives hold a great deal of uncertainty. There remains much more to be done to improve the living conditions of the refugees and also to support the Greek healthcare system at a time when Greece itself is struggling.

ASIA

JORDAN, IRAQ, AFGHANISTAN, PAKISTAN, INDIA, MYANMAR, MALAYSIA, SINGAPORE, HONG KONG, MONGOLIA, NORTH KOREA

MONGOLIA

NORTH KOREA

AFGHANISTAN

ASIA

HONG KONG

PAKISTAN

MYANMAR

INDIA

ARABIAN
SEA

BAY OF
BENGAL

SOUTH
CHINA
SEA

IRAQ

MALAYSIA

JORDAN

SINGAPORE

INDIAN
OCEAN

CHRONIC LIVER DISEASE IN AMMAN, JORDAN

DR MAISAM AKROUSH FRCP, CONSULTANT GASTROENTEROLOGIST AND HEPATOLOGIST

Chronic liver disease can be debilitating for the patient and the community, especially when it is coupled with a lack of knowledge. To address this issue, I was initially involved with the Ministry of Health hospitals in Jordan to set up a specialised hepatology clinic that provided care and information to patients.

In 2009, after I was elected as head of the scientific committee for the Friends of Liver Disease Society, public education became the major driving force of the Society along with sponsoring research in remote areas of Jordan where there is an obvious lack of medical facilities. To liaise between the public, including patient groups, and medical or government bodies, we also joined an organisation of other civil societies.

To promote awareness of liver disease, we took an aggressive approach to educate both the patients and the community at large. This involved informative lectures, training workshops and documentaries. I was also part of radio and television discussions about liver disease. We wanted to ensure that people understood not only how hepatitis viruses can be contracted, but also how that contraction can be prevented. Viral hepatitis had been taboo in the country because it could be

sexually transmitted. Many cases had been attributed to alcohol, even though this is rare in our part of the world. Our work involved setting up access to this information and eradicating the idea that there is no treatment for liver disease apart from sugar and complete bed rest.

People avoided those with liver disease as it was thought to be contagious, affecting job and marriage prospects. As one means of halting stigmatisation for liver disease patients, a liver support group was also established as a pioneer project. Here patients met and shared their personal experiences of various symptoms and treatments of the disease.

One positive outcome of the educational campaign was that new government regulations were put in place where blood banks had to inform donors that they tested positive for viral hepatitis. This was a major breakthrough as some people are unaware that they carry the virus and knowledge ultimately leads to better management of the disease.

My love for medicine grew with me throughout my childhood years culminating in 1989 when I completed high school exams gaining a spot in the top ten places nationwide. This effort

Women are still under-represented in the medical field. As a woman, I find that reaching the female population is easier and, in some cases, I am their voice in the community.

The author (far left) at a charity event to raise awareness (© Maisam Akroush)

was rewarded by a scholarship to study medicine at the University of Jordan.

Upon completion of my medical degree and further training in the Royal Medical Services, I received a scholarship in 2006 from the Jordanian Ministry of Health to complete training in the UK in internal medicine, gastroenterology and hepatology. During my scholarship, I passed the MRCP exams. Training and working abroad exposed me to knowledge that I brought back home with me to improve patient care.

In 2009, I passed the Jordanian Board of Gastroenterology and Hepatology exams, becoming the first female gastroenterologist and hepatologist in the country. It was not that difficult for me to be selected for a gastroenterologist post because the department knew me well as a previous internal medicine trainee. A much harder effort was needed to convince some male patients that their procedure would

be performed by a woman. For the first few years, my family also insisted on accompanying me if I had to see a patient in the emergency department at night. Travelling to conferences and meetings was initially criticised in the community but these attitudes changed, especially once more women entered the specialty.

Women are still under-represented in the medical field. As a woman, I find that reaching the female population is easier and, in some cases, I am their voice in the community. This is evident in recent work in Dubai Healthcare City, where we are able to ensure that the conservative lifestyle of some women does not limit their access to education and treatment.

As an honorary fellow, I act as liaison between the RCP in the UK and the Jordanian Ministry of Health, and we have signed a Memorandum of Understanding to allow specialist doctors from Jordan to be sent to train in the UK.

MEDICAL TRAINING IN IRAQ

PROFESSOR NIGEL BAX FRCP AND PROFESSOR DEBORAH BAX FRCP

King Hammurabi, who ruled Mesopotamia 4000 years ago, possibly introduced the world's first record of doctors' performance, with punishment for those who harmed patients. The Code of Hammurabi may be seen engraved on a basalt stele in the Musée du Louvre in Paris. Its principles are now part of many legal systems today and the discoveries in science and medicine that Mesopotamia, now Iraq, gave the world are core parts of our everyday lives.

Nine years ago, a telephone caller to the Academic Unit of Medical Education at the University of Sheffield asked: 'Can we come and talk to you about medical education?' The caller was Professor Hilal al Saffar, a fellow of the RCP, a cardiologist and head of medical education in the College of Medicine, University of Baghdad.

We went to see him and during our first visit to Baghdad we learned about the thousands of senior academics who had been under great personal pressure and in enormous danger along with their families. Unsurprisingly, many had left Iraq, and Iraqi medical education had been decimated. Indeed, we were very fortunate to be able to engage two of the refugees at our medical school in Sheffield: one was a professor of medicine and the other a professor of anatomy and surgery. What massive benefits we all gained from them.

We learned also of the collapse of English teaching in schools, of the lack of educational resources of all kinds and at every level, of the vast challenges

The Code of Hammurabi
(EmmePi Travel/Alamy Stock Photo)

We saw the dignity, resilience, tolerance and the huge abilities of the students and the staff of the medical colleges.

A pharmacy in Baghdad (© Nigel Bax)

facing universities in delivering teaching and of the difficulty faced by medical schools in providing clinical placements for their students. Postgraduate medical training was also in a parlous state. We saw the dignity, resilience, tolerance and the huge abilities of the students and the staff of the medical colleges. It was inspirational and humbling to see what was being achieved with little other than resolute determination. Even travelling to one's medical college in the morning and home later was a major undertaking requiring meticulous planning. One step out of line could end in disaster, as attested by the ten photographs hanging in a corridor just inside the entrance to the University of Baghdad College of Medicine, which commemorate members

of staff who were assassinated between 2006 and 2010. Even everyday clinical practice continues to have dangers, with incidents of patients' families and supporters threatening the life of the attending doctor. Despite all of this, and an uncertain future, recruitment to medical colleges is buoyant and the students are among the brightest and most committed one would meet anywhere.

Our work with the medical colleges and ministers has been in redeveloping medical curricula, seeking ways to support staff development, engaging with students and helping to develop thinking about how Iraq might regain its place as a centre of excellence in medical education, in which it was pre-eminent in the region only a few years ago. With Dr Jawad Rasheed, the Secretary General of the Arab Board of Health Specializations, we are introducing ways to support the development of trainees, initially through short academic and clinical attachments in Sheffield. In October 2016, Iraq was admitted as an Observer Member of the Union of European Medical Specialists. This will enable Iraq to contribute to discussions about medical training and provide access to training curricula in over forty specialties across Europe.

Hilal al Saffar has emphasised to the RCP the wish of Iraqi medicine to enhance educational, academic and clinical links with the United Kingdom and said how much Iraq would like Membership of the Royal College of Physicians clinical exams to be held there. A big but not impossible challenge! We all have so much to learn from each other.

MILITARY MEDICINE IN AFGHANISTAN

MAJOR DAMIAN JENKINS MRCP

The military medical facility at Camp Bastion began as a group of tents but had been replaced by a building of brick and steel by the time I arrived. It boasted a state-of-the-art emergency department, operating theatres, an intensive care unit, a mobile MRI scanner and a laboratory. It even had air conditioning to battle the 50°C desert heat.

UK military medical facilities are stratified into echelons: Role 1, situated close to the action, provides life-saving treatment, whereas Role 4 is sub-specialist care provided on home turf. In the middle, Role 2 and 3 facilities are capable of emergency surgical care and some specialist services. Camp Bastion was a Role 3 facility. Despite the emphasis on trauma, 'disease and non-battle injury' continues to account for the majority of ill health abroad – even in war zones – and where non-trauma illness springs up, so do physicians. Hence, in 2012, I found myself with a rifle and backpack over my shoulder, in south-western Afghanistan and engaged in Operation Herrick.

Staffing reflected the disease patterns of war: there were numerous surgeons of differing specialties, anaesthetists and a burgeoning cadre of emergency physicians and nurses. This mix of talents was commanded and cajoled by

A soldier is escorted by an RAF medic to a waiting ambulance, for a transfer to Camp Bastion (© Declan Walsh/IWM)

the non-medical staff of the deployed regiment. Here, in the midst of all this activity, and doing their best to be useful, were three physicians: a consultant each from the UK and the USA, and me, their neurology and medical registrar.

In a war zone, daily life is structured as much as possible. At the hospital, each day started with a ward round of all in-patients. The workload varied from, occasionally, no in-patients to providing physician-led care for half of the general ward. Mornings were punctuated by a hospital-wide discharge meeting, an important aspect of the routine work. The meeting was to ensure that the in-patients were kept to a bare minimum,

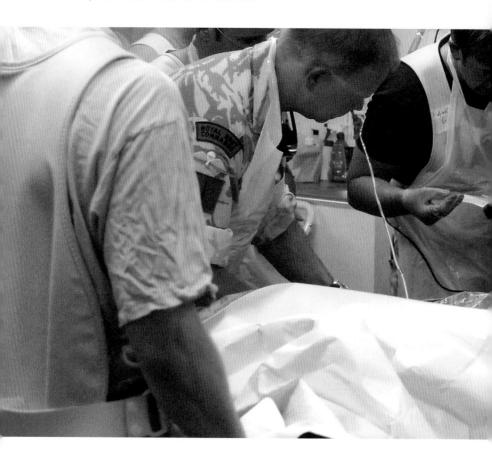

enabling us to respond to major trauma calls. After that I was on duty and I might be called to the emergency department or primary care. I might be asked to provide remote advice to personnel deployed elsewhere in Afghanistan or to see patients in intensive care. The day ended with a second ward round and a meeting with the medical director. Here we would be appraised of current military activity, because this inevitably dictated our workload. We would also get a report of the highest temperature of the day – something physicians liked to take bets on!

Being the only medical registrar, I was on-call 24 hours a day, seven days a week. As there was little else to do, this was not as burdensome as it sounds. Being resident on-call at night proved to be a real test of one's mettle: overnight working meant managing the emergency department and leading trauma calls, while awaiting surgical and anaesthetic consultants to arrive.

So what does a physician at war treat? In part this depends on the flow of trauma, which is prioritised above all else. However, the immediate population served in Camp

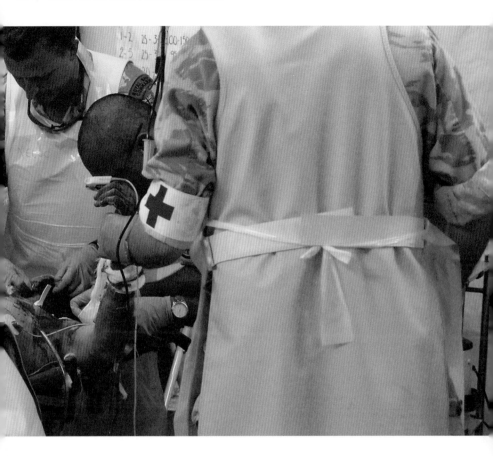

A casualty receives attention in the Emergency Department of the Camp Bastion Field Hospital
(© Crown Copyright/IWM)

Bastion varied from 5000 to 10,000 people and care was also provided to frontline troops, Afghan forces, enemy combatants and some civilians. As such, a surprisingly full range of medical ailments cropped up. Gastroenteritis and other infectious diseases made up the bulk of the work, but other conditions were also seen, such as disseminated intravascular coagulation from snake bites, renal colic and methanol poisoning. Indeed, we even helped during the delivery of Camp Bastion's first baby.

As a neurology registrar, to my delight, neurological presentations accounted for more than a quarter of admissions. Cases ranged from the usual (faints, fits and funny turns) to the less common (vertebral artery dissection, encephalitis and cluster headache) and to the tragic (glioblastoma multiforme and malignant multiple sclerosis). Also, children admitted to the general ward invariably fell to the care of physicians and this provided a steep learning curve, but was nonetheless rewarding.

To get to the position of on-call medical registrar in remote Afghanistan, I had trained for several years as an army doctor. This route took me through the Royal Military Academy in Sandhurst and then a medical officers course. Here I learned about the military and was trained in fieldcraft. I learned how to use weapons for both self-defence and the defence of patients. Finally, I was taught the essentials of trauma and emergent care, a skill set that was to prove invaluable once I had deployed.

In all, the time spent deployed in secondary care facilities in war zones was fulfilling and worthwhile. The medical ailments seen and the methods for dealing with them in resource-poor settings was helpful, providing a superb check on over-investigation and over-treatment. However, the real joy is the close-quarters working with a small, but highly skilled workforce. This forges friendships that last for life and provides for a wealth of stories, some of which are heart-rending, but many of which are heart-warming.

The real joy is the close-quarters working with a small, but highly skilled workforce. This forges friendships that last for life.

An ambulance waits to receive a casualty (MOD/Crown copyright)

PYRIMETHAMINE POISONING IN PAKISTAN

JAVED AKRAM FRCP

In 2011 I was the chief executive of Jinnah Hospital in Lahore, one of the largest hospitals in Pakistan. This was the culmination of a long journey which also took me to England for my general medicine training and MRCP diploma. After returning to my alma mater university, I became the principal there and then helped to run Jinnah Hospital.

In mid-December that year, patients from around the country started to arrive at our hospital with mysterious symptoms. They said that their complexion was darkening, they were extremely fatigued, they were bleeding easily and that they had fevers. We were all puzzled at the hospital.

A common factor seemed to be that they had fewer red and white blood cells (pancytopenia). On bone marrow biopsy, there was suppression of all cell lines in the patients. I had wondered about infections, but the patients were travelling from all over Pakistan and even neighbouring countries, such as Afghanistan. Lymphoma was also possible but would not explain the sudden occurrence in so many people.

One thing that struck me was that they were all patients with co-existing cardiac disease and I wondered about haemochromatosis, a condition of iron overload, which can lead to heart disease, liver disease, fatigue and pigmentation of the skin. However, the tests were negative for this too. To be honest, we were very confused, and two patients died during this time of uncertainty.

Jinnah Hospital (Asianet-Pakistan/Alamy Stock Photo)

In mid-December... patients from around the country started to arrive at our hospital with mysterious symptoms... we were all puzzled at the hospital.

The corridors of Jinnah Hospital (Asianet-Pakistan/Alamy Stock Photo)

After further delving into the history, we noted that all of the patients not only had heart disease but had also been receiving free cardiovascular medications from a single cardiology institute. They were on an average of six or seven medications, which were the same: a 'statin', a nitrate, an ACE inhibitor, aspirin and another anti-platelet drug. That was when we first wondered if a drug could be causing this.

I had to inform the Chief Minister of Punjab after other hospitals also reported patients with similar symptoms presenting to them. He asked me what should be done and I explained that we needed to rapidly analyse the implicated drugs in a specialist drug laboratory, as well as recalling the dispensed medications and alerting affected patients. An NHS laboratory in London kindly agreed to conduct such testing for us on an urgent basis. So, one of our staff with a valid UK visa flew to London with the patient histories and samples of the drugs.

Five days later, one of the drugs, isosorbide mononitrate, showed up an unknown ingredient on chromatography. Further tests identified the compound as pyrimethamine. When I was called with this information from the UK in the middle of the night, I immediately called the owner of the local factory that produced these isosorbide mononitrate tablets. It turned out that he also produced pyrimethamine for export to African countries.

It has made me keep my mind open whenever people present with unusual symptoms, and drug toxicity should always be in the differential diagnosis.

Pyrimethamine is a drug that is used in malaria prophylaxis and toxoplasmosis treatment. It inhibits production of tetrahydrofolate, essential for DNA synthesis and cell division, in most organisms including bacteria. In humans, it is taken with folinic acid to reduce side-effects and taken at a dose of about 50mg per week. Patients prescribed contaminated isosorbide mononitrate were ingesting up to 100mg per day. We now urgently administered the antidote, folinic acid, to as many of the 3000 affected patients as possible. Tragically, 151 people had already died by then, but there were no further deaths after folinic acid administration. It had taken nine weeks from the first presentation of the mysterious illness at our hospital to the administration of folinic acid.

Concurrently, we investigated how one batch of tablets became contaminated. It turned out that the pyrimethamine tablets and isosorbide mononitrate tablets were being produced in the same factory. Active ingredients should be coloured differently to prevent mistakes, but I found that both isosorbide mononitrate and pyrimethamine were almost identical white powders. I suspect that it was an inadvertent mix-up, which was then covered up and ignored.

A criminal investigation was launched and the factory's quality assurance personnel were arrested. Pakistani pharmaceutical companies export to over seventy countries and that business fell very sharply in light of the contamination that we uncovered. As a result, we now have legislation saying that active ingredients must be stored separately and coloured differently. Dedicated manufacturing areas exist for certain drugs to reduce the possibility of contamination, with drugs such as pyrimethamine being highly restricted. Quality checks are carried out more rigorously and we have our own spectrophotometer to help with this.

It has made me keep my mind open whenever people present with unusual symptoms, and drug toxicity should always be in the differential diagnosis. Scandals involving contamination have occurred in many countries, including the USA. One hopes that such crises never occur. If they do happen, there is nothing as rewarding as being able to help those most in need. The only silver lining in the incident was that we had managed to rescue thousands of people from likely death. That is the purpose of being a physician and my wealth is measured in my patients' hearts, not in the car I drive, the suit I wear or the house I live in.

MULTI-DRUG-RESISTANT TUBERCULOSIS IN MUMBAI, INDIA

DR ZARIR UDWADIA FRCP

John Crofton's former respiratory unit at the City Hospital, Edinburgh. Professor Crofton had first shown that the TB bacillus rapidly becomes resistant to treatment with one antibiotic, in his case streptomycin, and developed therapy using multiple antibiotics simultaneously. This is the mainstay of TB treatment even today.

During my days in the UK as a medical registrar we must have seen no more than a handful of TB cases in a year. Working in the TB clinic in Scotland often meant contact-tracing, in which we identified people at risk of TB from close contact with a patient, and cups of coffee to deal with the boredom. So, it was a huge culture shock when I returned after five years' training to become a young consultant to the Hinduja Hospital in Mumbai, and I found myself plunged into the maelstrom of TB that flourished in India. I set up a free weekly multi-drug-resistant TB clinic. At the time, in the early 1990s, the clinic was hardly busy, as multi-drug-resistant TB was relatively unknown globally.

Tuberculosis (TB) exists on an epic scale in India. It's difficult to be impervious to its presence. It remains India's biggest public health problem, resolutely refusing to go away. India has the highest population with TB in the world as well as the highest multi-drug-resistant TB population and there is one Indian death from TB every minute. These are grim statistics that have not changed over the decades.

I first arrived in the UK in 1988 as a lowly observer. There were none of the wonderful overseas training schemes that exist now and a job, any job, was hard to come by. After passing the MRCP exams, I trained in Professor Sir

Standard pulmonary TB is treated using a cocktail of four drugs, two of which are taken over a period of six months. If the organism is resistant to one of

ABOVE: A crowded street scene
RIGHT: Population density in India poses potential public health risks (both images Shutterstock)

India has the highest population with TB in the world as well as the highest multi-drug-resistant TB population and there is one Indian death from TB every minute.

the drugs, it is termed drug-resistant TB and multi-drug-resistant if two or more drugs are not effective. The spectrum continues with extensively drug-resistant TB with resistance to four or more different types of antibiotics. The increase in drug resistance in India was partly because detection and treatment of TB were not ideal. The one-size-fits-all approach didn't work. Patients were labelled as having TB when they had drug-resistant TB or they did not finish their course of treatment.

Over the decades, I witnessed first hand the relentless amplification of resistance, as we began to see large numbers of multi-drug-resistant TB, then extensively drug-resistant TB and finally the first cases in the country of totally drug-resistant TB. It was in 2011 that we identified four cases of patients who had TB that was resistant to all twelve drugs available for TB treatment. Often these patients had already undergone courses of TB treatment, including inappropriate regimens and antibiotics from private providers. On average, they had received nine drugs each for a duration of twenty-six months before we saw them.

The numbers seen in my clinic have swelled over the years and it is now the busiest outpatient department in the hospital with large numbers of patients, queuing up from across the country, desperately seeking a cure for their disease. These patients are termed by the Indian medical hierarchy as the 'no-hopers' and the 'untouchables' and have been caught between an exploitative private sector and a bureaucratic and uncaring public sector. What gives me pleasure and some degree of pride is that we have achieved success rates of around 70 per cent in these highly drug-resistant patients, a figure that is comparable with the best outcomes in the West, at a fraction of the cost.

OPPOSITE: A volunteer distributes food in a TB ward in Allahabad, Uttar Pradesh (ZUMA Press, Inc/Alamy)
BELOW: A public awareness campaign to combat TB in Hyderabad, Telangana (Shutterstock)

MULTI-DRUG-RESISTANT TUBERCULOSIS IN CHHATTISGARH, INDIA

DR EDWARD ARMSTRONG MRCP

The mobile clinic team in Chhattisgarh
(© Dr Armstrong)

After completing my core medical training and obtaining the MRCP exam I applied to work with Médecins Sans Frontières, an international medical charity. The application process was rigorous but achievable for RCP members with an interest in working in an international context. Soon after, I learned that I was successful and was asked if I would be prepared to work for nine months in the central Indian state of Chhattisgarh. After torrential flooding, an estimated 50,000 people had been displaced with no basic healthcare provision. Furthermore, the local population also suffered during an upsurge in violence between the state's security forces and regional insurgents.

Our project aimed to provide health services for the local population affected both directly and indirectly by the conflict. This covered primary care, acute care and management of infectious diseases, such as TB and malaria. In addition, we held health education sessions, antenatal checks and a childhood vaccination programme.

As part of my initial training, I spent one week at another aid project in Mumbai focusing on the management of patients co-infected with HIV and drug-resistant TB. Bringing this specialist knowledge back to our project was beneficial in improving our systems for diagnosing and managing our own patients. We discovered that over a dozen of our patients were infected with drug resistant TB. Some of them came on foot and lived several hours away from our clinic. If we suspected the disease, then sputum samples would have to be delivered to the nearest airport in Hyderabad, which was seven hours

Washing up after a clinic team outing along the Godavari river (© Dr Armstrong)

by car, and then flown to a reliable reference laboratory in Mumbai for drug resistance testing.

The logistics of then providing treatment to these patients were extensive. They would need regular medication and check-ups over a continuous period of up to two years. We worked in a remote rural region with no formal roads, no running water, no health clinics, no pharmacies and no mobile phone network. The terrain was often only accessible by foot, especially during the heavy monsoon season. Also, the flare-up in the regional conflict sometimes resulted in areas becoming out of bounds due to safety concerns.

Furthermore, we had to educate and counsel patients appropriately regarding the importance of adhering to their medications, despite side effects and their living circumstances. Where possible, we trained a community health worker to be able to directly observe treatment and ensure medications were taken. However, for those people living in inaccessible areas, we had to rely on additional health education sessions. Nevertheless, we monitored treatment adherence in this group and partly because of the greater sense of community involvement in treatment, the rates of medication adherence were not lower than in people being directly observed.

Our team and our health education advocates on the project showed great dedication and motivation in the face of these challenges. It was personally inspiring for me to witness that the majority of our patients completed treatment and were eventually cured, demonstrating that through a sustained commitment it was possible to provide drug-resistant TB treatment in even the most remote areas.

THE MRCP EXAMINATIONS AND YANGON GENERAL HOSPITAL, MYANMAR

DR THET NAUNG MRCP

Every morning I wake up, have a bath and eat breakfast. After paying my respects to Buddha, I begin work as a medical officer at Yangon General Hospital.

Usually I work for over eight hours in a day or night shift and am one of about eight interns in the medical admissions team that may admit up to 200 patients on days when we are on duty. Of course, nurses are also busy and one nurse may care for over twenty-five newly admitted patients. The more senior doctors oversee this and also run clinics in which they see another 200 patients in a day. I receive no salary but volunteer to do this to receive teaching and experience at the hospital.

I have wanted to practise internal medicine since my medical school days in Yangon because I believe internists will have a crucial role in improving the health of the country's population. To help fund my revision and exams, I earn money from working in my spare time as a medical officer in a private hospital and by tutoring undergraduate medical students for their own exams. During 2016, I was also revising for the MRCP PACES exam.

The exam is important to me for two reasons. Firstly, Myanmar is now a rapidly developing country with more international investment and personnel in healthcare. Having the MRCP exam is a benchmark that guarantees my professional skills internationally, since there is no similar domestic exam. Secondly, I would like to join the Medical Training Initiative, which was set up by the RCP to allow doctors like me to gain internal medicine experience in the UK.

This experience abroad would be invaluable for my future practice. For example, haemodialysis is rarely used currently in end-stage renal failure although physicians recommend it and it is offered free of charge for the first few times. Also, intravenous alteplase is available but there is no training or

OPPOSITE: The exterior of Yangon General Hospital
ABOVE: Yangon's citizens praying at Shwedagon pagoda (Both images © Krishna Chinthapalli)

funding for an acute stroke thrombolysis service. The new government, elected in 2015, will hopefully change things, and by the time I am a senior physician these treatments may be much more widely used. We have voted for a new government to invest more into healthcare and raise healthcare standards for everyone. After finishing my own training, I want to practise as an internist to be able to help the greatest number of sick patients and diseases.

YANGON GENERAL HOSPITAL
KRISHNA CHINTHAPALLI

Yangon, also called Rangoon, is a bustling city of temples, markets and five million people. They have recently been joined by fast food outlets, shopping malls and luxury hotels. Along the road from the gleaming windows of one mall and a new American fast-food outlet with doormen outside, is Yangon General Hospital. It is an imposing Edwardian building of red brick and yellow plaster, constructed over a century ago, when Yangon was twenty times smaller than it is today.

When it opened in 1909, the 320-bed hospital had incorporated the latest advances in hospital design, such as anaesthetic rooms next to operating rooms, reinforced

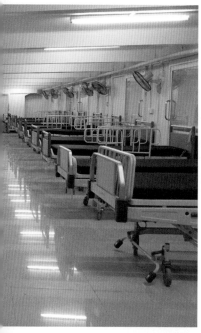

concrete floors and open 'Nightingale' wards with large windows and balconies to allow fresh air in.

Now, there are over 1500 inpatients in beds crammed again the walls and even the balconies of the building. People make their way to the hospital from smaller towns and villages too, not just from Yangon itself. One doctor describes the hospital's catchment area as the whole country. The public are increasingly aware of Yangon General Hospital having a reputation as the best public hospital and admissions have more than doubled in the last ten years. Prospective patients often bring their own bed, their relatives to help care for them and, most importantly, money to pay for medicines, food or even intravenous contrast for scans. Scans are not always available – the hospital has the only public MRI scanner in the city, with three others available in private hospitals. On the other hand, expertise is provided by 300 doctors in all areas except obstetrics.

Aung San Suu Kyi formed a committee in 2012 to renovate this hospital. She recognised that the 'historic and iconic building has been providing care for the people of Rangoon for 115 years and it is in serious need of maintenance'. Thus, the Rangoon General Hospital Reinvigoration Committee has been raising funds and looking at how to reduce demand and increase supply. For example, it has recommended developing referral pathways so that patients with illnesses such as gastroenteritis are treated at local hospitals. It has helped the hospital to expand to 2000 beds and added new departments, such as hand microsurgery. Information stations are being set up to guide visitors and patients can even complain about poor service using a dedicated phone line. The hospital is once again on the frontline in leading hospital and secondary healthcare improvement in Myanmar.

ABOVE: Thet Naung (far right) with colleagues in Yangon General Hospital
TOP: A ward nearing completion in a new extension of the hospital. (both images © Krishna Chinthapalli)

HYPERTENSION IN MALAYSIA

PROFESSOR YOOK CHIN CHIA FRCP, PRESIDENT OF THE MALAYSIAN SOCIETY OF HYPERTENSION

Malaysia is a diverse country of thirty million people, who are of Malay (67 per cent), Chinese (25 per cent) and Indian (7 per cent) origin. The economy is in transition and, along with rapid urbanisation, there has been the adoption of the so-called 'unhealthy lifestyle'. This lifestyle has contributed to the high prevalence of cardiovascular risk factors: 30 per cent of adults are overweight, 35 per cent have high cholesterol and 33 per cent have hypertension. Malaysia already has the highest obesity rate in south-east Asia. By 2011, diabetes prevalence had risen from 8 per cent to 20 per cent in just fifteen years. It is not surprising that cardiovascular disease now accounts for a quarter of all deaths in the country. With an ageing population and increasing prevalence of risk factors, the burden of cardiovascular disease will only rise.

Hypertension is a particularly serious issue not only because it is common, but also because of the lack of awareness about it. In the 2006 National Health and Morbidity survey, adults underwent screening of blood pressure. About 64 per cent of adults were not aware that they had hypertension and, by 2011, this figure had dropped only to 61 per cent. Among adults who had known hypertension, 87 per cent were receiving medications. Unfortunately, even in these patients, hypertension was adequately controlled only in 26 per cent..

A clinic in rural Sarawak (© Professor Yook Chin Chia)

Hypertension is a particularly serious issue not only because it is common, but also because of the lack of awareness about it.

World Hypertension Day exhibition for raising awareness (© Professor Yook Chin Chia)

The Malaysian government and the Malaysian Society for Hypertension, of which I am president, have taken steps to improve this. Public education on a healthy lifestyle has been widely promoted but may be of limited effectiveness. Recently, there have been efforts to reduce salt intake in the population. The Ministry of Health is engaging food manufacturers to label the salt content in their products and a number of products, such as instant noodles and soya sauce, already have less salt content now. The government has also made all drugs for hypertension, including expensive proprietary combination pills, easily available in primary care.

The Malaysian Society for Hypertension has also raised awareness among doctors. Doctors are encouraged to check blood pressure in routine clinic visits. Indeed, some practices now have a nurse to take readings using an automated blood pressure monitor as patients wait. On World Hypertension Day 2015, screening for hypertension proved to be very successful and cost-effectiveness analysis by the Society suggests that screening for hypertension may be worthwhile, with a cost of about US$2.68 per person newly diagnosed with hypertension.

In recent years, cardiovascular mortality rates appear to have started falling. However, Malaysia still has an age-standardised mortality rate of 296 per 100,000 population, whereas neighbouring Singapore has reduced it to 108 per 100,000 population. Malaysia is fortunate to have good infrastructure and a public healthcare system that is largely free and accessible for most people. More work is needed not only by the government but also by every individual and healthcare professional to build on our progress.

I initially trained in internal medicine and first became interested in hypertension in 1993, when I conducted a community survey of 1400 people in Kuala Langat, a semi-rural area eighty kilometres from the capital city, Kuala Lumpur. At the time, cardiovascular disease was thought to be a disease of Westernised and developed countries. I was told that it was not a big issue in Malaysia. However, my survey revealed that cardiovascular disease was just as prevalent in these patients as it was in developed countries.

After training, I was asked to help set up a department of primary care and started helping with drug trials in hypertension. Since then, I have continued to manage people with hypertension and cardiovascular disease. For me, it has been rewarding to see that effective monitoring and management has reduced the mean systolic blood pressure from 148 mmHg to 138 mmHg and mean HbA1c (glycated haemoglobin) level from 8 per cent to 7 per cent in my patients. I have seen the effect of this, with far fewer patients suffering from strokes, blindness or kidney failure.

A view of the countryside near Kota Kinabalu on the island of Borneo (© Professor Yook Chin Chia)

INFORMATION TECHNOLOGY IN HEALTHCARE IN SINGAPORE

DR THOFIQUE ADAMJEE MRCP

ABOVE: An ambulance in Singapore (iStock)
OPPOSITE: Supertree Grove (Manfred Gottschalk/ Alamy Stock Photo)

Torn between taking my first consultant job in the UK or in Singapore, I opted for the unknown. It has now been over two years here and it has been a fabulous experience. On first arriving, I learned to cook and in the process relished the wonderful local fruits (such as mangosteens, custard apples and rambutans) as well as classic Singaporean hawker market dishes.

Once I started work a few months later, as an associate consultant in Internal Medicine, I was won over by the hospital, which is a stunning and functional building with gardens and ponds. It also has a refreshing 'can-do' attitude to quality improvement and innovation. Internal medicine is an established standalone specialty here and, unlike the UK, I frequently manage conditions from arthropathies to epilepsy relatively independently – a steep but enriching learning curve. The government is keen to shift the tide away from patients seeing several super-specialists towards a generalist-led service with specialty in-reach.

I am now setting up an Acute Medicine service here to help improve patient

A local food hall (robertharding/Alamy Stock Photo)

It has taken time for me to adapt to the expectations of patients here. Older Singaporeans frequently defer decisions regarding their health to their children and wish to know little themselves.

safety, reduce length of stay and restore generalist medical care to the forefront. The funding model in Singapore makes ambulatory emergency care more challenging. In-patient care is deductible from one's health savings account, which is accrued from salary deductions, but all out-patient and ambulatory care is paid out-of-pocket. However, I hope to work with the Ministry of Health to find a way to work around these financial disincentives. It has been fascinating to learn to practise medicine differently when patients are paying for all treatments from their account and this has forced me to be even more careful and pragmatic with tests or treatments. I now know the exact costs of medications and scans.

It has taken time for me to adapt to the expectations of patients here. Older Singaporeans frequently defer decisions regarding their health to their children and wish to know little themselves. This has been challenging at times, as families frequently demand that I withhold a serious diagnosis from patients and expect to be updated of results before the patient is told. When covering for colleagues during the two-week Chinese New Year holidays, I found that many families were also superstitious regarding death, which is unlucky in the New Year, and did not wish to discuss end-of-life care.

Language can be a big challenge too. I was assured that Singapore's administrative language is English and that language would not be a concern. However, the older generation includes a mix of Tamil, Mandarin and Malay speakers (all official languages) plus several who speak only dialects such as Hokkien and Teochew, meaning much can be lost in translation.

Efficiency is one of the stereotypes of Singapore, but even so I was amazed in my first week to see self-driving robots delivering hot meals to each ward. Critical laboratory or radiology results are automatically routed via text message to the primary physician or the on-call doctor's

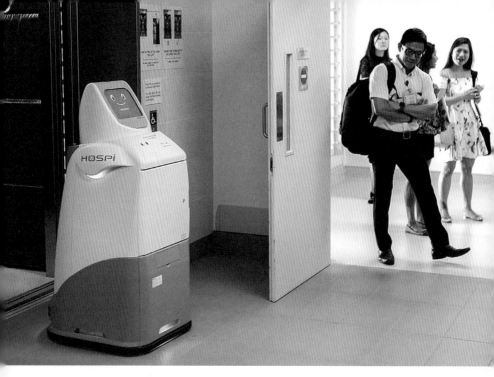

Panasonic Autonomous Delivery Robots – HOSPI – aid hospital operations at Changi General Hospital (© Panasonic)

mobile phone. Patients and expensive equipment can be tracked via wireless tracking devices so they don't go missing. All patient observations are wirelessly integrated onto the electronic health record. Another luxury is that all internal and external CPD points are automatically logged centrally from attendance lists, so the local equivalent of the RCP CPD Diary is auto-populated and downloadable at the end of the year.

Conversely, one of the biggest healthcare challenges in Singapore is primary care. Patients seek out a public or private GP themselves and commonly shop around various different GPs with little continuity or ownership. There has long been a need for a complete medical record and recently the National Electronic Health Record (NEHR) has been successfully implemented.

The NEHR is a work in progress, with the vision of 'One Singaporean, One Health Record'. Everyone living in Singapore has an ID card which allows a single health record to be attached to their Identity Card Number. Doctors can view medications, allergies, diagnoses, lab and radiology reports, discharge summaries and appointments. These are pooled from most healthcare providers. We can even see if the treatments have been dispensed or not, giving a clue to compliance. Private sector GPs and hospitals are also on board with the NEHR, and it is now even accessible from some nursing homes. The most recent addition allows patients to access their results, discharge summaries and appointments via a secure online portal. This is an IT project that other countries can only dream of for now.

CIGARETTE SMOKING IN HONG KONG, MONGOLIA AND NORTH KOREA

DR JUDITH MACKAY FRCP, SENIOR POLICY ADVISOR, WORLD HEALTH ORGANIZATION

I studied medicine at the University of Edinburgh and have lived in Hong Kong since 1967, initially working as a hospital physician. In 1984, I decided to concentrate on the broader issues of prevention and public health policy, especially tobacco control.

This was precipitated by three things. First, hospital wards in Hong Kong were crammed with smokers. In fact, there had been a saying that the male wards never admitted a non-smoker. I realised that hospital medicine was like a sticking plaster; prevention was essential to improving health via the corridors of political power, not the corridors of hospitals and clinics.

Second, I was interested in women's issues and health. This was very gynaecologically defined in those days and I realised that, actually, more women were dying from tobacco. Girls and women were being exploited and aggressively recruited by tobacco companies, whose advertisements featured attractive, slim, successful

OPPOSITE: A Chinese cigarette advert, 1930s
(Chronicle/Alamy)
ABOVE: The RCP's Smoking and Health report was influential around the world, and especially in Asia
This is the Japanese edition (© John Mackay)

The tobacco companies denounced me as 'entirely unrepresentative and unaccountable', contrasting themselves as 'identifiable, legal, accountable, commercial organizations' ... it was a turning point in my life and the fight was on.

ABOVE: Warnings on cigarette packets. The enlargement of the size of pictorial health warnings to 85% of the cigarette pack area came into effect in Hong Kong in June 2018 (© Hong Kong Council on Smoking and Health)
OPPOSITE: North Korean soldiers smoking (Eric LAFFORGUE/Getty Images)

women and promised emancipation, when tobacco addiction is just another form of bondage.

Third, between 1979 and 1981, I wrote a series on health in the *South China Morning Post*. In response to four tobacco articles, the tobacco companies denounced me as 'entirely unrepresentative and unaccountable', contrasting themselves as 'identifiable, legal, accountable, commercial organizations'. That was it. It was a turning point in my life and the fight was on.

There was no career structure for working in tobacco control in Asia in the 1980s, and no funding agencies. My medical training hadn't included my new duties: framing tax arguments in lobbying Ministers of Finance, answering cross-examination in court by tobacco industry lawyers, making public health newsworthy, negotiating international UN treaties like the World Health Organization's Framework Convention on Tobacco Control (WHO FCTC), or navigating free-trade disputes and litigation. Single-handedly and self-taught, I developed extensive experience in all these areas, working with national governments and health organisations in Asia to develop more comprehensive tobacco control policies.

This work is surprisingly similar in either the largest (China) or the smallest population countries in the world (some Pacific Islands); in different political systems of kingdoms, democracies or communist states; in countries at very different stages of economic development; and countries with a national tobacco monopoly or international tobacco companies. It is the same product, same harm, same obstacles and same actions that need to be taken. The tobacco industry also operates surprisingly identically in marketing its product and obstructing effective government action on tobacco control.

There has been a sea change in Asia since 1984, showing that tobacco control is not the prerogative of Western countries. Singapore enacted the earliest tobacco

A Chinese anti-smoking campaign (Francois LE DIASCORN/Getty Images)

control legislation and ban on duty-free cigarettes. Hong Kong was the first to ban smokeless tobacco. Thailand innovated the use of tobacco taxes to fund health promotion. Several jurisdictions (Hong Kong, Japan, Singapore) have halved male smoking prevalence rates over the last forty years and, to date, the expected increase in female smokers has not materialised.

I'm still particularly interested in tobacco and women, tobacco control policy in low- and middle-income countries, the economics of tobacco, trade issues, and exposing and resisting challenges by the tobacco industry, which remains a tough adversary. My work continues to take me across the world. Recently I provided guidance on combating the growing tobacco epidemic in the Eastern Mediterranean region. The FCTC, major donors like Bloomberg Philanthropies and resources like *The Tobacco Atlas* (which I co-author) provide today's advocates with the support and tools I lacked in 1984 – helping to accelerate global progress. Ultimately, I'd like to see every country ratify FCTC and fully implement and enforce its measures to deliver a healthier, wealthier, tobacco-free world.

THE IMPACT OF DR MACKAY'S WORK

KRISHNA CHINTHAPALLI

In 1881, when the modern cigarette was invented, James Duke exclaimed 'Bring me the atlas!' He leafed through the pages, glancing at the population figures until he stopped at China: 430 million people. Triumphantly, he pointed and said 'That is where we are going to sell cigarettes.' His company later became British American Tobacco and pioneered cigarette sales in China by the 1890s. A century later, four out of ten cigarettes worldwide were sold in China. This was the backdrop when Judith Mackay gave up her job in 1984 to become the first person in Hong Kong to fight full time for tobacco control in the province, and then the rest of Asia.

In 1990, Mackay was one of the first advisors to arrive in Mongolia within days of the democratic revolution. She had been invited to draft a national tobacco control framework. She thinks that being a woman from the UK meant the government, along with many others in the region, found her less threatening and also politically neutral. Nevertheless, the new health ministry prepared educational workshops in schools for her to visit and was surprised when she instead asked their staff numerous questions about tobacco imports, tobacco taxation, fires caused by smoking and so forth. Such was her persistence that the health minister held a cabinet meeting to discuss whether she could be a spy. They decided not in the end. She had not escaped danger though: on an evening stroll from the government guesthouse she was held at gunpoint by Mongolian palace guards who had no idea who she was. Near the end of the trip, the health ministry asked her to go ahead with writing a tobacco control law. She finished her draft after staying up all night before catching her flight out of Ulaan Bator in the morning. That draft was the basis of Mongolia's comprehensive tobacco legislation passed four years later.

In 2012, Mackay went on holiday to North Korea. Officials there discovered that, ten years earlier, she had helped veterans of the country's famed 1966 World Cup football team fly to England for a reunion. In gratitude, they granted her access to health officials and since then she has been back regularly to advise them on introducing smoke-free areas and increasing the price of cigarettes.

Mongolia and North Korea are just two examples. Out of six WHO regions, the Western Pacific is the only one in which all countries have ratified the FCTC. It is also Judith Mackay's home. That is no coincidence.

Such was her persistence that the health minister held a cabinet meeting to discuss whether she could be a spy.

OCEANIA

AUSTRALIA

ARAFURA
SEA

CORAL
SEA

NT

AUSTRALIA

QLD

WA

OCEANIA

SA

NSW

GREAT
AUSTRALIAN
BIGHT

VIC

DIVING MEDICINE IN AUSTRALIA

DR CARL EDMONDS MRCP

Like many Australian medics, I went to the UK for postgraduate training after a period as a 'flying doctor' in Western Australia, following my graduation. En route, I stopped in Hawaii and one day, when the sea was too calm to surf, I was introduced to scuba diving. After three years I could no longer tolerate the weather in the UK and so returned to Australia – to surf, sail and scuba.

In Australia, I joined the Underwater Research Group, then the Royal Australian Navy School of Underwater Medicine. Here I founded civilian diving medical centres and the South Pacific Underwater Medical Society.

Basic hyperbaric physiology had been clarified by researchers in the early twentieth century, but it was after the Second World War that scuba diving gained popularity. Sophisticated diving equipment permitted greater exposures, often distant from medical support. New environmental and equipment-based illnesses arose in otherwise fit young adults – divers with whom I worked and dived – and were unrecognised by their physicians. Medical discoveries were inevitable, especially in the diveable tropical and semi-tropical waters of the Indo-Pacific.

Perhaps our earliest influence was on diving otology and we found that many cases of inner ear damage were due to barotrauma. More interestingly, we collected many cases of disorientation while diving and investigated these with the newly introduced electronystagmography. We introduced an extensive classification of

Diving medicine has undergone huge changes over the decades. This image shows a British Navy diver in a decompression chamber, 1945 (General Photographic Agency/Stringer)

TOP: A member of an Australian dive team sits in a decompression chamber
MIDDLE: An Australian Navy Seaman prepares to conduct explosive ordnance cleaning off the coast of the Solomon Islands
BOTTOM: Attending to a casualty in the decompression chamber (All © Royal Australian Navy)

diving-induced vertigo and hearing loss in a textbook in 1973. After this I was conscripted to the US Navy and NASA (for the space programme) but was mistakenly identified as an otologist.

A deluge of decompression sickness cases occurred in the context of pearl, abalone and computer-based diving and required prompt treatment. Until the 1960s, the only treatment for decompression sickness was in a hyperbaric chamber but most of the places that recreational divers went to did not have one. Divers could not be transported in time to the nearest chamber and ended up becoming permanently disabled. Therefore, in 1971, I introduced on-site underwater recompression treatments. A diver with decompression sickness was lowered underwater in a harbour, with water acting as a natural hyperbaric chamber, and supplied with hyperbaric oxygen without nitrogen. This emergency technique spread worldwide, with modifications, and is now in the US Navy diving manual.

One major challenge for Royal Australian Navy medical divers was to identify and treat any new diving illness in the navy or for civilians. If there was a death, we often did not know the cause, even after testing the equipment. Therefore, we would re-enact the dive with the same equipment and even with a person of similar size, but with a companion diver. Often, accidents were due to equipment failure that we had not appreciated and could be confirmed with tests, such as gas samples checking for hypoxia. We had medical back-up but even so this was a risky procedure that we performed only when no cause was known. Thus, we clarified the causes of many deaths or illnesses, including those misnamed by divers as shallow water blackout, oxygen syncope or sea water fever. Investigation of diving deaths took much of our time and led to us formulating specific autopsy procedures for diving deaths. This also allowed us to define the various causes and recommend prophylaxis and medical standards for diving. Other clinical breakthroughs involved sinus barotraumas, saltwater aspiration syndromes, long-term effects of diving, neuro-psychological syndromes and reverse dive profiles.

There were also marine animal injuries. The taxonomy and toxicology was well documented, but although fascinating to marine biologists, this was not so helpful to patients. Our divers were frequent victims and I toured the Indo-Pacific to record the clinical data and medical treatments available. After publishing our information on dangerous marine animals, I was now mistaken for a marine biologist.

All of the information gained was the basis for another textbook, *Diving and Subaquatic Medicine*, in 1976. The latest edition in 2015 was five times larger, showing the advances made in the field. My last major contribution to diving medicine was in 2016, my octogenarian year, after a decade of studying the deaths of middle-aged women with sudden pulmonary oedema during diving. The cause appears to be Takotsubo cardiomyopathy. Now, my diving activities are limited to snorkelling and I have retired (almost).

An underwater safety stop, being observed by ascending divers to avoid decompression sickness (Shutterstock)

NORTH AMERICA

THE MARSHALL ISLANDS AND THE USA

MARSHALL ISLANDS

PACIFIC
OCEAN

CHINA   MARSHALL ISLANDS

AUSTRALIA

UNITED STATES
OF AMERICA

NORTH AMERICA

NORTH
PACIFIC
OCEAN

NORT
ATLAN
OCEA

GULF OF
MEXICO

DIABETES MELLITUS IN THE MARSHALL ISLANDS AND THE USA

DR PETER GOULDEN FRCP, ASSISTANT PROFESSOR IN ENDOCRINOLOGY AT UNIVERSITY OF ARKANSAS FOR MEDICAL SCIENCES

Having arrived in Arkansas in the southern USA in late 2012, I knew immediately that my role as the Endocrinology Medical Director in the state's sole academic centre had great potential to serve those most in need. That led me to pilot work with the under-served population of the Arkansas Delta, a rural area bordering the Mississippi Delta. This work led to a US$2.2 million study with the Arkansas Marshallese.

Marshallese lady cooking on a traditional coconut stove (Travel Pix/Alamy)

The Marshallese are a people from the Marshall Islands in the South Pacific. They are from a population that experienced low rates of diabetes until many of its people were forced to relocate to the USA after nuclear weapons testing on their islands in the 1940s and 1950s. At first, a small number of the Marshall Islanders moved to Arkansas with job offers from a poultry firm with headquarters here. They were then joined by other fellow citizens and now there are over 12,000 Marshallese people in the region – the most outside their country.

The sudden move from a fish- and plant-based diet to the Western staple foods led to a rapid rise in diabetes, with a prevalence of about 50 per cent in adults. This high rate of diabetes, occurring in a population without adequate access to healthcare, was the spur to the current project:

bringing diabetes education to the doorstep. Unlike previous attempts, this is based on a model in which the team meet and engage with the whole family, sometimes in their homes, and successfully making a positive change.

I now lead a diabetes clinic for this population using a combination of new point-of-care technology, with real-time glycated haemoglobin, serum creatinine and urinary albumin results, coupled with face-to-face interaction. This project has opened my eyes as an endocrinologist as to what is important in diabetes care and has been one of the most rewarding chapters in my career. It is a chapter which I hope will lead to better diabetes care and reduced complications for this population.

My interest in medicine began in the small town of Keighley in Yorkshire and led to my studying medicine at the University of Edinburgh. From the works of one of the university's most well-known graduates, Dr Arthur Conan Doyle, I realised that applying the forensic logic of Sherlock Holmes can serve the clinician well – with careful communication skills. My interest in endocrinology was born on the old Nightingale wards of the Edinburgh Royal Infirmary as a junior house officer with the inspiring clinicians of the endocrine firm. As a consultant in endocrinology, my focus was on education and I served as an RCP tutor for five years, working to develop and expand core medical training in my hospital. I combined this with the role of regional diabetes lead in my region and published abstracts annually to maintain the academic focus.

After a fortuitous meeting with the chief endocrinologist at the University of Arkansas for Medical Sciences, I decided to move to the USA in 2012. My future in the USA lies in building excellence in patient care in endocrinology and serving those most in need. I also continue to help the RCP as an International Advisor.

Reflecting on my journey from those early days in the old Edinburgh Royal Infirmary, I realise that the common theme has been education and enquiry, both for myself and the patients I serve. Indeed, when in doubt, I turn to the words of a former University of Edinburgh graduate: 'When you have eliminated the impossible, whatever remains, however improbable, must be the truth.'

TOP LEFT: Blinded by diabetes, a man learns to walk again with a stick (Heather Charles/*Chicago Tribune*/MCT via Getty Images)
TOP RIGHT: Checking blood sugar in Washington, DC (*The Washington Post*/Michael S Williamson/Getty Images)
OPPOSITE PAGE: Marshallese leave Bikini Atoll, 1946 (Carl Mydans/The LIFE Picture Collection/Getty Images)

The Marshallese are from a population that experienced low rates of diabetes until many of its people were forced to relocate to the USA after nuclear weapons testing on their islands in the 1940s and 1950s.

SOUTH AMERICA

BOLIVIA

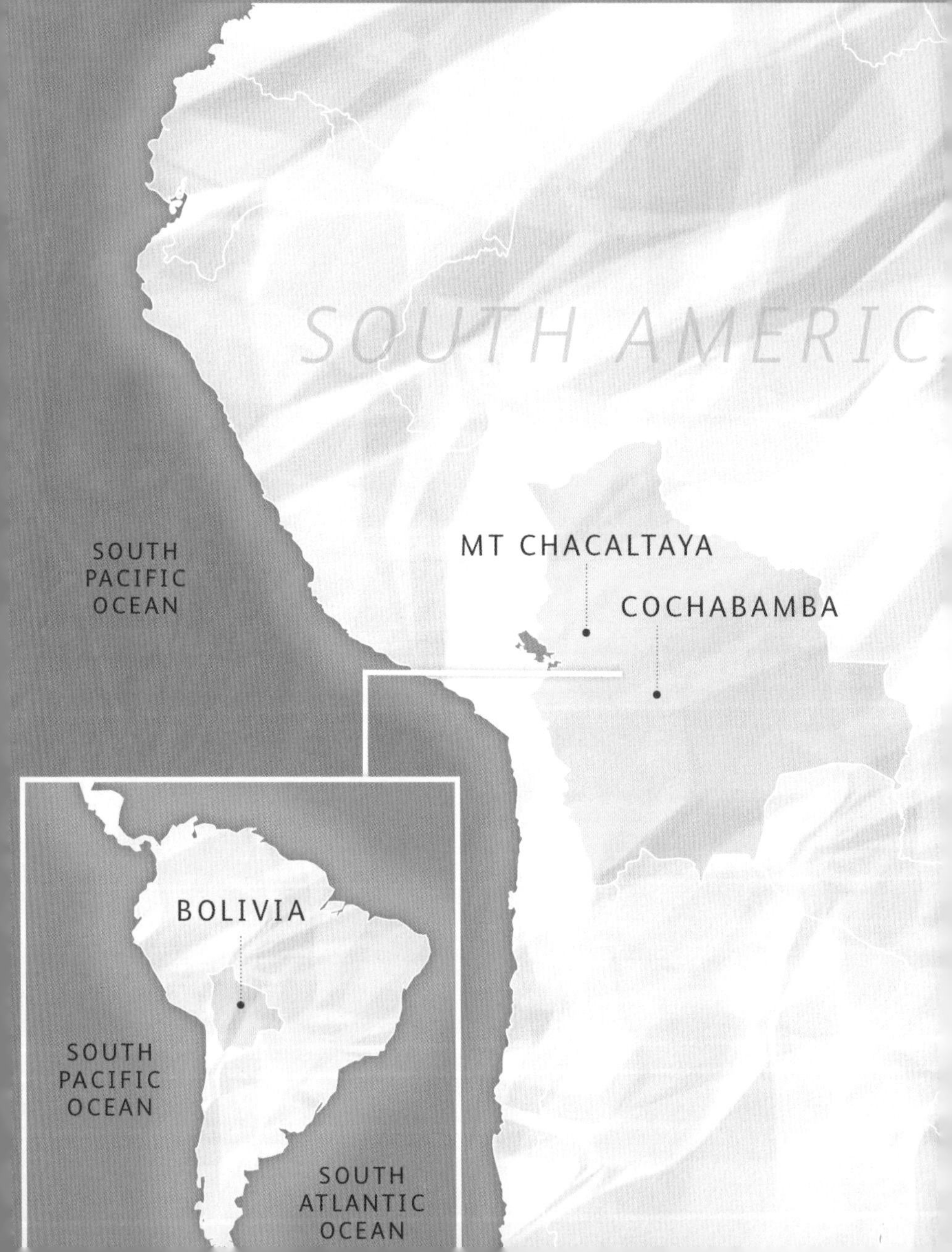

SOUTH AMERIC
SOUTH PACIFIC OCEAN
MT CHACALTAYA
COCHABAMBA
BOLIVIA
SOUTH PACIFIC OCEAN
SOUTH ATLANTIC OCEAN

CHAGAS DISEASE IN COCHABAMBA, BOLIVIA

PROFESSOR DAVID MARTIN FRCP, ASSOCIATE INTERNATIONAL DIRECTOR, RCP & PRESIDENT, PROJECT PACER INTERNATIONAL

My country is the world, all mankind are my brethren, and my religion is to do good.
THOMAS PAINE

For the last twenty-five years I have had the pleasure of participating in medical work focused on the provision of sustainable cardiac therapies for patients with Chagas disease in Cochabamba, the third largest city in Bolivia. This work is conducted under the auspices of a Boston-based charity, Project Pacer International, which was set up to help people around the world benefit from advances in cardiac electrophysiology. Our care is delivered in partnership with our hosts at Viedma Hospital and Universidad Mayor de San Simon, to whom we owe a large debt of gratitude for their generous hospitality.

Bolivia is a landlocked South American republic with a long colonial history followed by more than 200 coups d'état before the establishment of democracy in 1982. This has resulted in deep-seated poverty and a lack of social cohesion, which is reflected in its health service.

ABOVE: Prof David Martin and Drs Yoel Vivas and Jaime Arandia (Bolivia) planning a case to be conducted in the catheter lab behind the group
BELOW: Villagers from a remote area (with high prevalence of Chagas disease) arrive by chartered truck to the hospital. (both images © Project Pacer International)

The additional burdens of extensive corruption and participation in the illegal drug market have prevented social progress at a time when most other South American countries have seen economic growth; for example, while Brazil has eliminated more than 98 per cent of vector transmission of *Trypanosoma cruzi*, Bolivia has had no such success and there are areas of the country (particularly in the Cochabamba department) where the prevalence of seropositivity for *Trypanosoma cruzi* is 50 per cent of the population. Since approximately 20 per cent of seropositive patients develop cardiac complications of chronic Chagas disease, there remains a large population at risk and therefore the need for advanced cardiac therapies such as pacemakers and defibrillators remains very high.

The success of Project Pacer International's mission in Cochabamba is related to its core principles. First, we have a strong commitment to the poor and try to ensure that all work is focused on the truly indigent; Viedma Hospital social workers screen all patients and the hospital applies a variable fee schedule for the use of procedure rooms and hospital beds. Although we provide all pacemakers and other implantable devices as well as antibiotics and local anaesthetics free of charge, it is not possible within the Bolivian healthcare system for even the poorest patients to avoid making some contribution to their care.

Second, we focus on the application of sustainable therapies providing a clear benefit: we have avoided prescription of medications that we cannot provide for patients on a long-term basis and have devoted our core activities to procedural work where a single intervention (pacemaker implant, radio frequency catheter ablation, or balloon mitral valvuloplasty) can provide tangible and long-term benefit to patients in terms of quality of life and economic productivity.

A local woman at a typical market scene in Cochabamba (© Project Pacer International)

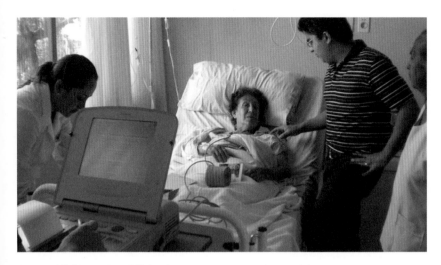

Yoel Vivas MD (Venezuela and USA) explains post-operative wound care and discharge instructions to a patient after pacemaker implant (© Project Pacer International)

The third principle is that the quality of care delivered in a resource-poor environment must be comparable to that delivered in our home institutions; we work hard to ensure that all members of our team are highly skilled and experienced, and that they have the temperament necessary to work productively in challenging circumstances. The quality of care is also critically dependent upon strong working relationships with the local professional staff and we have been delighted with the close and highly effective bond that has developed between our Boston-based team and the group based in Cochabamba.

The maturity and consistency of this relationship with our hosts requires much ongoing effort but is highly rewarding in that we are able to efficiently take care of a large number of patients in a few days. During a typical week of work at Viedma Hospital our group sees 300 new patients, a similar number of patients with implanted devices requiring maintenance, and performs approximately sixty device implants, twelve catheter ablations, and six mitral valvuloplasties. While our teams may be present at Viedma Hospital for only a few days per year, it is possible for communication regarding patient care and device troubleshooting to occur at any time.

During our time in Bolivia, to help support the high volume of sterile procedures requiring fluoroscopy, we have supplemented the local infrastructure by shipping various cardiac monitoring machines to the hospital.

Finally, a core element of our work has been education and professional development. The learning that occurs during this work is bi-directional: teams of physicians from

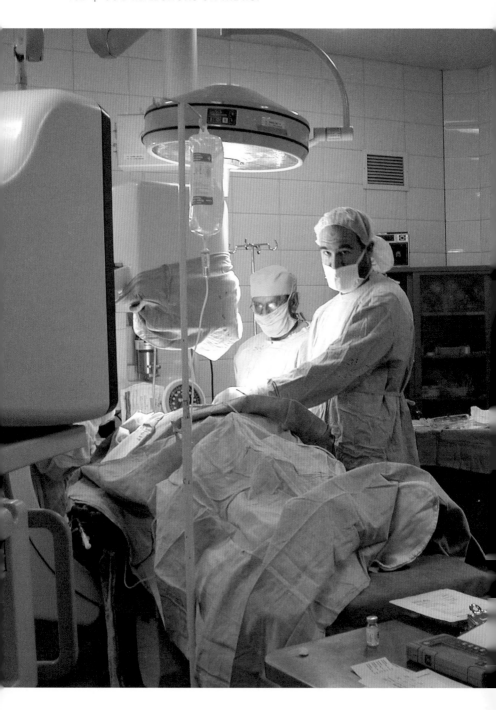

some of the most sophisticated healthcare systems in the world always come away from this experience with a newfound appreciation for the range of possibilities in care provided in resource-poor settings. Our work routinely involves the teaching of local physicians, with both side-by-side work in the procedure rooms as well as more didactic discussions in a formal conference setting in which we tend to learn as much from our hosts as they learn from us. We also regularly travel with medical residents and cardiology fellows from our home institutions in the US and we encourage our trainees to work with their Bolivian counterparts. In an increasingly interconnected world such educational opportunities for US-based trainees is seen by them as invaluable and highly beneficial to their future practice.

The basic human needs for water, nutrition, sanitation, immunisation and obstetric care are well understood but are commonly unmet in parts of the world. The work of our team in a technology-dependent subspecialty of cardiology makes a big difference in Bolivia, where a burdensome parasitic disease continues to ravage the population and the country's potential.

Cardiovascular surgeon Dr German Garcia (Bolivia) and Kathleen Malewicki, RM (USA) during pacemaker implant at Viedma Hospital operating theatre. (© Project Pacer International)

The basic human needs for water, nutrition, sanitation, immunisation and obstetric care are well understood but are commonly unmet in parts of the world.

ALTITUDE RESEARCH IN MOUNT CHACALTAYA, BOLIVIA

DR ROGER THOMPSON MRCP

ABOVE: Dr Roger Thompson (©
Alistair Simpson)
OPPOSITE: The base for the
research, a physics laboratory on
Mount Chacaltaya (© Olivia Swann)

Why do scientists and clinicians climb high up mountains in remote locations, despite freezing temperatures and a lack of access to shelter, running water or a power supply? It is at least in part human curiosity – and the desire to better understand human responses to hypoxia, including how maladaptation results in potentially fatal altitude illnesses. In Bolivia, Altitude Physiology Expeditions (Apex) has utilised a cosmic physics laboratory, run by the Universidad de Mayor San Andrés, La Paz, and the adjacent Club Andino building, the world's highest ski lodge, to overcome some of the logistical problems involved in altitude research. The buildings stand near the summit of Mount Chacaltaya at 5240 metres above sea level (asl), in a spectacular setting amidst the Andes. Only two hours from the Bolivian capital and easily accessible by a dirt track road, this location has provided a safe research base for four expeditions by Apex since 2001. Our participants are volunteers, mostly undergraduate students from the UK, with no recent history of altitude exposure. After flying to the world's highest capital city, La Paz, at 3650m asl, and acclimatising for four days, volunteers ascend by road to Chacaltaya.

There are three important altitude-related diseases. Acute mountain sickness (AMS, a common self-limiting syndrome of non-specific symptoms), high altitude pulmonary oedema and high altitude cerebral oedema (both less common

The project team ascends Mount Chacaltaya
(© Alistair Simpson)

With millions of people travelling to high altitude each year to ski, trek and climb, education about the risks of altitude hypoxia remains a priority.

than AMS but potentially fatal conditions). Our model of controlled, non-exertional ascent induces AMS in approximately 70 per cent of participants. We have published research showing that systemic oxidative stress occurs at high altitude, but that prophylactic oral antioxidant supplementation did not prevent AMS in a randomised controlled trial. More recently, analysis of visual analogue symptom scores identified at least two distinct syndromes of symptoms associated with ascent to altitude, implying that AMS may not comprise a single disease process and suggesting a need for reassessment of the existing consensus diagnostic criteria.

Driven by successive generations of enthusiastic medical students and junior doctors with developing interests in altitude and expedition medicine, we have continued to organise research expeditions. We also promote awareness of altitude pathology on a website and through regular public engagement activities in the UK. With millions of people travelling to high altitude each year to ski, trek and climb, education about the risks of altitude hypoxia remains a priority, while ongoing research attempts to find new ways to improve acclimatisation and eliminate serious diseases.

An optional undergraduate study module in 2000 completely transformed my medical career, when I was asked by Kenneth Baillie, a fellow student, to help set up a research expedition. The hook was simple: the project would be about altitude medicine and the location would be Bolivia. While I knew nothing about altitude research at that time, I was quickly consumed by the appeal of designing and conducting research in a field setting and the challenge of organising an expedition. With enthusiastic support, we set up an experiment looking for a link between high altitude cough threshold and the response in ventilation to carbon dioxide. Although we found no correlation, the project sparked my interest in altitude research. Indeed, the months spent recruiting volunteers, securing sponsorship and finalising logistics prior to the first Apex expedition failed to deter me from taking charge of a second expedition two years later, immediately after completion of my first year as a doctor.

Apex 2 comprised several groups of volunteers arriving in Bolivia for a randomised controlled trial of antioxidant supplementation and sildenafil. The willingness of the volunteers to participate in the research despite the effects of AMS was truly admirable. Equally the help and support of the Bolivian locals, notably the manager of the hostel in La Paz and the drivers who provided us with a twenty-four-hour service, was invaluable. Leading the expedition was a hugely rewarding experience with perhaps the greatest privilege simply being part of such a committed, enthusiastic and friendly group of people. Since then, the Apex mantle has been taken on by students aware of previous Apex work but with fresh and independent desire to pursue unsolved mysteries of altitude pathology.

While I remain involved in encouraging and helping others to organise Apex expeditions, my own research interests have gradually evolved alongside my clinical career as a respiratory physician. Hypoxia continues to be an important theme of my work and my current focus is on how hypoxia and inflammation influence pulmonary blood vessel remodelling in the context of sea-level diseases. Given that altitude hypoxia also induces reversible remodelling in these blood vessels, it would certainly not be surprising if my future research led me to return to Bolivia and to the highest lab in the world.

A portable Gamow bag used to treat a single occupant with altitude-related pathology. The pressure inside the inflated bag is higher than ambient atmospheric pressure. (© Alistair Simpson)

ANTARCTICA

SOUTH
ATLANTIC
OCEAN

HALLEY VI RESEARCH STATION

INDI
OCE/

ANTARCTICA

SOUTH POLE

ANTARCTICA

SOUTH
PACIFIC
OCEAN

SOUTH
PACIFIC
OCEAN

RESEARCH IN THE BRITISH ANTARCTIC TERRITORY

DR RICHARD CORBETT MRCP

Halley is the southernmost of the British Antarctic Survey research stations and is one of only two permanent British research stations to sit within the Antarctic Circle. The current station (Halley VI) is the latest in a series of incarnations since the first station was built in 1956. Its primary role is the delivery of environmental research science, specifically atmospheric sciences, glaciology and space weather. Much of the work is long-term data collection; the importance of this is underlined by the station's role in the 1980s in identifying the hole in the ozone layer based upon observations collected since the station's inception.

A field trip to the nearby Emperor penguin colony
(© Richard Corbett)

The year has two distinct austral seasons of summer and winter, though even during the summer it is uncommon for temperatures to rise above 0°C, while in the winter temperatures frequently dip to below -50°C. The summer lasts for no longer than three months, during which time the station population may swell to around seventy people, and twenty-four-hour daylight allows a large amount of work to be undertaken. Such work includes scientific field expeditions, station maintenance and resupply of essential goods. For the remainder of the year, there are sixteen individuals (including a doctor), who are effectively physically isolated from the outside world and have to be self-sufficient. This includes three months of winter, in which the sun never rises above the horizon and the station is frequently buffeted by 50 knot (90 km/h) winds. The nearest research station is several hundred miles away across crevasse-ridden ice fields and impenetrable weather.

It is this physical isolation that creates the biggest challenge to the station doctor. Indeed it is often remarked that it is easier to return an injured astronaut from space than it is to retrieve personnel in the Antarctic winter. Nonetheless, the medicine is rarely challenging and as suited to a physician as much as any specialty.

The Halley research station (© Richard Corbett)

The skills acquired in pre-deployment training to act as dentist and radiographer for the respective midwinter dental checks and occasional broken bone are called upon more frequently, thankfully, than those of anaesthetist or surgeon. Moreover, the well-stocked surgery provides for the equally highly improbable but nonetheless challenging prospect of the first presentation of diabetes or tuberculosis that would otherwise be life-threatening in a remote setting.

I worked across two summers and a winter during 2006–08, as well as being a ship's doctor on the long voyages in and out, having realised since my medical school elective that an interest in tropical medicine was incompatible with my preference for an environment where the ambient temperature is -30°C rather than +30°C. Despite the paucity of clinical work, there was plenty of need for help assisting in many of the other roles needed to keep a research station running smoothly, from covering the chef to flying the first unmanned aerial vehicles in the Antarctic. There was also time to run human physiological research projects. The prolonged darkness means that it is an ideal location for research that is not only informative about the role of bright light in circadian rhythm entrainment, but is also a paradigm for other environments where access to natural light is limited or impractical, such as submarines or space.

The medicine may bear little comparison to my current job as a renal physician but teamwork is central to both roles, often under challenging circumstances. As well as having worked with a motivated and close-knit group of individuals, I was very fortunate to have witnessed a stunningly beautiful and unspoilt area of the world, which is threatened by the onslaught of global warming and the destructive effect of humans on the environment.

It is often remarked that it is easier to return an injured astronaut from space than it is to retrieve personnel in the Antarctic winter.

BIBLIOGRAPHY

THOMAS LINACRE

G. Clark, *A History of the Royal College of Physicians of London*: Volume one, 1964, Clarendon Press: Oxford.

J. F. D. Shrewsbury, *A History of Bubonic Plague in the British Isles*, 2005, Cambridge University Press.

Munks Roll, http://munksroll.rcplondon.ac.uk/Biography/Details/2752

J. Woolfson, *Padua and the Tudors*, 1998, University of Toronto Press: Toronto.

HANS SLOANE

S. A. Hawkins, 'Sir Hans Sloane (1660–1735): his life and legacy', *Ulster Medical Journal*, 2010; 79(1): 25-29.

THOMAS HODGKIN

M. J. Stone, 'Thomas Hodgkin: medical immortal and uncompromising idealist', Proceedings Baylor University Medical Center, 2005; 18: 368–375.

PATRICK MANSON

P. Manson-Bahr, *Patrick Manson: The father of tropical medicine*, 1962, Nelson: London.

HELEN MACKAY

D. Stevens, 'Pride, prejudice, and paediatrics (women paediatricians in England before 1950)', *Arch Dis Child*, Oct 2006: 91(10): 866–70.

E. M. Poskitt, 'Early history of iron deficiency', British Journal of Haematology, Aug 2003: 122(4): 554–62.

Treatment of podoconiosis is based on reducing contact with the soil . . . There are large numbers of affected people who will not be cured now but we aim to prevent new cases, especially in young people. With continued funding and advocacy, I hope to see the elimination of the disease within our lifetimes.